SELECTED LYRICS
BY ED FRAM

Selected Lyrics
by Ed Fram

Ed Fram

F E FRAM

Contents

1

(Section One) A feelin' too far

The day has come a-stormin'
into the dark room of my mind
Facin' another mornin'
thinkin' of who I've left behind
But you always said it true
I could never be with you
We're just one feelin' too far
from where you and I both are ...

The engines are still a-roarin'
The ship's battlin' with the waves
And the rain don't stop pourin'
Like the tears you never forgave
But you always said it true
I could never be with you
We're just one feelin' too far
from where you and I both are ...

It's a senseless, empty searchin'
Tearin' apart the bad from the good
Singin' without a branch for perchin'
The song don't sound like it should
And you always said it true
I could never be with you
We're just one feelin' too far
from where you and I both are ...

© Ed Fram 2015

2

A stranger unmet

It's written my son
You have to move on
With time to forget
A stranger unmet

But babe I lay down, I lay down for you
Though you were only passing through
Like an angel surrendering his wings
Like the bended grass saluting the winds
Now they say in your grave you wept
You wept to extinguish the fires of regret

And it's written my son
You have to move on
With time to forget
A stranger unmet

You said that door will lead me to nowhere
The old self I'm searching, he ain't really there

So tell me, why have you still got the key?
Don't you see, you're just different shades of me?

For it's written my son
You have to move on
With time to forget
A stranger unmet

© Ed Fram 2015

3

A tear I gave you

A tear I gave you, don't you recall?
I loved too easily, my true downfall
Some want sweet, some seek long-haul
Some are made to fall on the sword like Saul

A tear filled with grief, too heavy to fall
I drag this load like a laden lead ball
Two bodies, one coffin to the resting hall
In time with the bells of Saint Paul

A tear yet felt and formed to fall
Look out, it'll come like a tidal wall!
To wash away one and all
Separating vacant voices from His call

A tear so silent says it all
The wailing wind, this black shawl
Whispers of hope in ears so small
Giants cut down, on their knees they crawl

A tear gives life like the rain that falls
Black is but a colour and that's all
The sunken ship will make landfall
In time with the bells of Saint Paul

A tear I gave you, don't you recall?
I loved too easily, my true downfall
Some want sweet, some seek long-haul
Some are made to fall on the sword like Saul

© Ed Fram 2016

4

A thousand moons

Can we be cursed for caring
too deeply for the damned?
Who shall bear the blame for us belated finding
what's always been written in Heaven's own hand?

The foxes shiver near yesterday's princes,
weeping their blue blood.
The Judge's hand shan't quiver to deliver sentences,
to those beyond the final flood.
Now look 'tween the sweet flow of ol' time's river
and a flower that blooms.
There shall be cast the stone low, reaching hither;
where all must wither before dawn be day, brighter than
a thousand moons.

Come set fire to the aborted rain!
Shred the secrets soon to be whole!
The target's ready for aim,
return the seat that you stole!

For not one stone shall be ruined,
in the making of this smile.
But explaining the moods of the wind,
may yet take a little while …

"No one will love you like me" the serpent speaks clear as
virgin frost of dawn.
"No one could love me like you" I mutter as though to repent, so hollow and forlorn.
But the gift that taketh from the weary,
will some day run its course.
When called to riseth combined to query,
the truth seekers come in force.

Can we be cursed for caring
too deeply for the damned?
Who shall bear the blame for us belated finding
what's always been written in Heaven's own hand?

© Ed Fram 2018

5

Above my weeping wall

They say that time's a healer
It'll take away any hurt feelings
But that just makes it a stealer
And leaves me staring cold at ceilings
Sometimes it comes easy and rhyming
Sometimes it don't come at all
But I know your light's always shining
Above my weeping wall ...

They say that a man who talks alone
Is a sign of a mind gone wrong
But if you look for what's been shown
You might find he was right all along
Sometimes it comes easy and rhyming
Sometimes it don't come at all
But I know your light's always shining
Above my weeping wall ...

They say the deepest meaning can be found in the shal-
lowest of wells
Where beggars lie naked, never able to choose
But be careful not to mistake their simplicity for the
spoiler's spells
And remember the last to laugh has the most to lose
Sometimes it comes easy and rhyming
Sometimes it don't come at all
But I know your light's always shining
Above my weeping wall ...

© Ed Fram 2015

6

At Charlie's

The dreamer and the dreamed about
In common they got nearly naught
But the caged and the bird that flew
Ain't they kinda like me and you?
And the singer and the sung for
Their song won't be heard no more

Over at Charlie's café
Charcoal crowd chasing dusty blues away
And Charlie, he's readying the pipe
He's thinking he knows my type
I'll just have some tea, actually
All ain't what you see, Charlie ...

Ah but people, oftentimes they say
I wouldn't let myself get that way
I only hope they never touch this day
'Cos takes a mile or a few in these sandals
To know what you can and can't handle

Over at Charlie's café
Charcoal crowd chasing dusty blues away
And Charlie, he's readying the pipe
He's thinking he knows my type
I'll just have some tea, actually
All ain't what you see, Charlie ...

The dreamer and the dreamed about
In common they got nearly naught
But the caged and the bird that flew
Ain't they kinda like me and you?
And the singer and the sung for
Their song won't be heard no more

© Ed Fram 2016

7

At the brightness of the dawn

If you're seeing your way past the storm
Through wind and snow clouds so brave
Know that she'll be there to take you in so warm
For who else would you pray the date to save?
The girl who was there at the brightness of the dawn
Will be there when the night calls upon your grave ...

Now see that you hold her so tight
She can't be the one you let get away
Her cares next to yours are so light
But what can ever make you stay?

The tenderness you miss in her smile
You found in the letter from her that day
She wrote "we've not met in a while
But I feel your love, it'll never pass away"

"Old love must make way for the new
They say you're spoken for now"
"How can you believe what isn't true?
Come back to me, we'll make the vow"

If you're seeing your way past the storm
Through wind and snow clouds so brave
Know that she'll be there to take you in so warm
For who else would you pray the date to save?
The girl who was there at the brightness of the dawn
Will be there when the night calls upon your grave ...

© Ed Fram 2015

8

Ballad of a boy

Baby show the way
To when I was a boy
All fun without no pay
Bring me back my joy

Time went before it came
My heel before my hand
I even changed my name
I wrote it in the sand

A father's tomb for reference
Mamma's light for show
Pick your poison of preference
And guess the way to go

Time went before it came
Death ahead of life
You loved me just the same
But I never made you my wife

Stars are fighting over space
I just wanna hug you tight
I was never born to race
I just wanna do you right

Time went before it came
A cure before the curse
There's no one left to blame
Not a penny in my purse

Baby show the way
To when I was a boy
All fun without no pay
Bring me back my joy

© Ed Fram 2016

9

Be my baby tonight

Love me like it's gonna last
be my sunlight in the night
Feed me like it's the eve of a fast
and be my baby tonight

Hurt me like you care too much
My time ain't yours to lose
let me ache for your kiss and touch
But don't make me choose

Thrill me like the early days
How our joy knew no end
Now just actors in washed-up plays
Baby, let's stop playing pretend

Lead me to the other side
Back to our youth, where the dreary passed us by
We'll kiss lips that never lied
For love is born of truth and true love can never die

(Forever love is born of truth; true love can never die)

Love me like it's gonna last
be my sunlight in the night
Feed me like it's the eve of a fast
and be my baby tonight

© Ed Fram 2018

10

Before the heart starts to harden

In you, I found more to praise than to pardon
Not much of a hand to raise, I'll just throw my best card
in
With little skill and less flair, the rest ain't got a prayer
Come back with me, under the willow tree there
We can talk Bacall, Bogart and Monroe
And all the films they never starred in
And all the sweet places we could go
Before the heart starts to harden

You see I've been here before, so let's make this day count
All butterflies, honey and more,
before the knight in your mind must dismount
The silver river, it leaves a bit of itself at each turn
Gather the gold from autumn leaves that wither
Let that forgotten tree yearn
For talk of Bacall, Bogart and Monroe

And all the films they never starred in
And all the sweet places we could go
Before the heart starts to harden

Walk me to the tomb to the sound of my own tune
I'll doff my cap and say good afternoon
To you or anyone that'll make it come soon
The heart is filled, it can do nothing but break
So call in the choirmaster, I'll see you at the wake
Beside the weeping tree, to be a burning stake
To recall Bacall, Bogart and Monroe
And all the films they never starred in
And all the sweet places we could go
Before the heart starts to harden

© Ed Fram 2020

11

Blanket of tears

As the tree stands naked
Upon its blanket of tears
I'll look at what I've rated
As the hour draws near

Slipping away aside the Spanish stone
Always sickened by the cure
With pain my pal calling me home
I know gold won't heal the poor

So I'll send out the searching team
Another attempt to find myself
His walk's the same it seems
But they got somebody else

My baby and I, we swapped locks
But we never shared a key
I hear he's handed you a rock
But will he make you happy?

I'll be gathering the ashes of a life past
Just another avowed ascetic
A poet raking the fields of pain at last
You said it was rather pathetic

They say you can't kill time twice
So you'd better make it count
If another hand shakes the dice
Would it show the same amount?

Like the tree standing naked
Upon its blanket of tears
I'll look at what I've rated
As the hour draws near

© Ed Fram 2016

12

Blood price

"Chivalry's dead!", the feminist read
to the cardboard drifter, who's living just to figure out
why he's not dead
Claim your pew, I won't be far behind
The Lord's right next to you,
He don't need to ask what's on your mind
Now there's no place to hide
No place to run from sun or shade
There's no use taking a look inside
The blood price has already been paid

The throngs come, just to see me standing alone
Wishing they're the one, I'll be taking home
Now I don't wanna be with anyone else, I just can't be
with you
Love's a law unto itself, you always knew I was only pass-
ing through
Now there's no place to hide
No place to run from sun or shade

There's no use taking a look inside
The blood price has already been paid

I was struck down by His words, a breath of music to the
ears
But the mystery seeker, she can't believe what she hears
With her diamonds languishing mid-air off her lobes like
chandeliers
Far away, the wild cry of a childless mother
And my silence knowing you belong to another
Still there's no place to hide
No place to run from sun or shade
There's no use taking a look inside
The blood price has already been paid

To the other, please send him my regards
For company all I got is a box of cheap cigars
Across the street, the red lights flicker
Never to fill all those empty baskets of wicker
So don't agonise over choosing a bridge
It's the same side you'll be landing, with nothing but
dreams to discourage
But will the girl's ghost be forever where you're standing?
Now there's no place to hide
No place to run from sun or shade
There's no use taking a look inside
The blood price has already been paid

This old river we all know, it don't need your tears to
flow

There's trouble at every turn of history's pages
It flows, filled with the sadness of bygone ages
Every leaf has a time to grow and a time to fall
Every soul a season to sow and a season to heed the
Lord's final call
Now there's no place to hide
No place to run from sun or shade
There's no use taking a look inside
The blood price has already been paid

© Ed Fram 2020

13

Darkness and Desire

The tree with your hand 'twas sown, now all green and
grown
But its shade will never touch you, the birds can't call it
home
The bookkeeper watches over complexity and simplicity
in a duel
Fighting over knowledge, who's wearing a crystal clear
jewel
While darkness is silently missing the sound of the stars
And desire is defiantly beating to a tune that was never
ours ...

The artist is no man's fool, he knows his white from his
black
So why are you lying to him, before he even turns to look
back?
The paintings are on the wall, ambition is in the drawer
The cruelty of compromise has war joining the peace
corps

While darkness is silently missing the sound of the stars
And desire is defiantly beating to a tune that was never
ours ...

The tormented traveller, he has nowhere left to wander
So you must carry on alone to that place, yonder
Where sex is forbidden among dreams of undying fame
Where only the eternal infant and tired egos remain
And darkness is silently missing the sound of the stars
While desire is defiantly beating to a tune that was never
ours ...

© Ed Fram 2015

14

Destiny on ice

Too many masters to serve
He knows you can't kill him twice
We all want to deserve
To drink from our destiny on ice

He traded from evil East
out to the wicked West
At your mercy, at the feast
Selling nothing but the best
He has no time for the truth
And no ability to lie
Always a liability in his youth
Forever asking why

Different answers, but question's still the same
A lie can reveal more than the truth they claim
Forgetting your lines won't stop the play
Somehow the poor man's still gotta pay

He traded from evil East
out to the wicked West
At your mercy, at the feast
Selling nothing but the best
He has no time for the truth
And no ability to lie
Always a liability in his youth
Forever asking why

But this truth, it can fade
From the Count and the self-made
Not knowing how the cards will fall
The only way out, is never to get in at all

He traded from evil East
out to the wicked West
At your mercy, at the feast
Selling nothing but the best
He has no time for the truth
And no ability to lie
Always a liability in his youth
Forever asking why
Too many masters to serve
He knows you can't kill him twice
We all want to deserve
To drink from our destiny on ice

© Ed Fram 2019

15

Eden's sunrise

Now the path I'm a-travellin', it chose me long ago
Though all seemed mapped out, a time to hide 'n' a time
to show
But even the mariner is lost at sea, see how lost the wise
can really be
And the master, he's just sittin' here strokin' his mous-
tache at me
All the while a-wonderin', how I dared pick an apple
from his tree ...

But I'm here to see the secrets, before they're all too well-
known
Here to drink it up, before the cup bringin' life has over-
flown ...

For the breakthrough always comes, before the first fruit
falls to the floor
"Can't you see I'm doing you a favour my Lord, the solu-
tion is two-score"

"Well, I knew that all along boy, now tell me what you
waitin' for?
Truth can't forgive and forget, to keep a-knockin' on a
bolted door
She needs to know why she's here too, you might as well
pick some more!"

So if you want to see the secrets, before they're all too
well-known
Be sure to gather up the harvest, before the seed of sin's
been sown ...

But remember those who are last will be first, the first
last
It'll happen in the future, though it's a lesson from the
past
Now who's standin' where, it's hard to tell with the lines
all blurred
Some are claiming victory, before a starter pistol's even
been heard
But you can know your placin', without utterin' another
wasteful word
Listen to the worshippin' whispers of the prayerful, filter
out the absurd!

And be there to see the secrets, before they're all too
well-known
Be there at Eden's sunrise, before the garden is again dis-
own'd ...

16

Faye

Get fat, get thin
Get a job and a home to live in
Turn to dust, get a stone
Let the grievers groan and moan
If I should go this very day
Cry not for me, my darling Faye

Take this flower
Lay it upon thy grave
It holds the power
To free and enslave
Each petal a parable to guide the way
Only follow from afar, my darling Faye

In the library of the living
The great book stands
Loving and forgiving
All it commands
Rules there are ten, clear to obey

We'll meet again, my darling Faye

Our minds will melt
Into a crucible of cares
At the crucifix we knelt
For the sacrifice He dares
And if we should go this very day
Cry not for me, nor my darling Faye

© Ed Fram 2016

17

Home again

In the dawning half-light
Of our congested sprawl
Glimpse the crow mid-flight
And see me giving it my all

I ain't got a penny
But you make me feel like a millionaire
Fame - i ain't got any
But wherever we go people stop and stare

When the door slams
Windows open silently
She's another man's
She whispers to me softly

I ain't got a penny
But you make me feel like a millionaire
Fame - i ain't got any
But wherever we go people stop and stare

A sunset so crisp and clean
A child's smile so pure
No greater joy has there been
You coming back to me once more

© Ed Fram 2019

18

It's all coming true, (though it ain't in view)

You won't be coming back here, no need for lookin' be-
hind
You can't call after her, the name has slipped your mind
The ghost of your child is reaching out a hand
Crying red tears and demanding you take a stand
The blind man's vision is moving beyond you
And it's all coming true, though it ain't in view ...

The streets ain't safe after the birds have flown
Gather up all the cages you used to own
The mayor on the steps of the town hall
Is throwing crazy curveballs at your wall
The floor, too, is dancing under you
And it's all coming true, though it ain't in view ...

Leave experience to be the educator for another fool
You learnt the job well, but now they want a different
tool
The nameless one is standing at your shore,
Taming the tide and calling you back for more
But your ship is still sailing out into the blue
And it's all coming true, though it ain't in view ...

All your steely sellers, they are taking stock
Their chains are busted, no use for locks
The joker who's laughing at your door
Has his arms around the one you adore
Give them a wave, it's time to say adieu
And it's all coming true, though it ain't in view ...

© Ed Fram 2015

19

Just to be moving

News of your leaving
Went further than you ever did
He held your hand
While the rest thought you'd hid
But I knew you'd go back
Back to the old man's farm
As the whisky slid
I never meant you no harm
But she ain't just your kid

Sometimes I wonder if you miss me at all
But I can't help you tear down that wall
Baby, I loved you mighty good
Sure, I coulda lent a hand like I said I would
Maybe multi-tasking like Roland Kirk
Back then, it seemed too much like hard work ...

The good go sideways
Just to be moving

The bad go any which way
Long as you're believing
That ugliness wins the day
And tomorrow never conquered
An enemy it could not foresee
If you knew what you do now
Would it change your reality?

Still, sometimes I wonder if you miss me at all
But I can't help you tear down that wall
Baby, I loved you mighty good
Sure, I coulda lent a hand like I said I would
Maybe multi-tasking like Roland Kirk
But back then, it seemed too much like hard work ...

© Ed Fram 2017

20

Last tomorrow

Whatever way we go
It ain't ours to know
If today was our last tomorrow
There'd be no time for sorrow
There'd be no time for sorrow

And like words on a page
Tired of saying the same thing
You told me the world's a stage
Only if you have a song to sing

Whatever way we go
It ain't ours to know
If today was our last tomorrow
There'd be no time for sorrow
There'd be no time for sorrow

So pack up your cares
Blindly follow the dark

Mind the broken stairs
Ignore the shattered arc

Whatever way we go
It ain't ours to know
If today was our last tomorrow
There'd be no time for sorrow
There'd be no time for sorrow

Worn are the feet that tread
To your notes of liquid lyre
Upon ancient streets they led
I'd go on but for fire
Yes, I'd go on but for fire

Whatever way we go
It ain't ours to know
If today was our last tomorrow
There'd be no time for sorrow
There'd be no time for sorrow

© Ed Fram 2016

21

Les neiges d'antan

Twisted tales pass for news
Transfixed but bemused
With the social stains of the lonely
There's beauty in pain
So says Leonard Cohen
Between cries of Stella I'm bleeding

Yesteryear's snow, in rivers it flows
Changed but not forgotten
But when tomorrow's winds blow
Will it be back clean as cotton?

I love you still
I'll love you until
I love you only
By then you'll see
It's only me
That you're needing

Yesteryear's snow, in rivers it flows
Changed but not forgotten
But when tomorrow's winds blow
Will it be back clean as cotton?

The flower asks not the reason
As the sun sets the season
There's beauty in confusion
Like ancient souls in modern times
We fill our minds
With ideas that need feeding

Yesteryear's snow, in rivers it flows
Changed but not forgotten
But when tomorrow's winds blow
Will it be back clean as cotton?

© Ed Fram 2016

22

Mama's pearls

I knew our lives would be together woven
Like the plaits you wore as a little girl
Though but a boy, the heart had chosen
For you to look after mama's pearls ...

I'll take my fast feet to nowhere, I'll take them out of sight
With these hands busy but empty of power
I'm struck down by the moonbeam light
But your purity before the midnight hour
Tells me it'll all be alright...

Lovers' dreams carried on gondolas by candlelight
Ancient melodies chiming from each bell tower
Lost to time all those last kisses goodnight
But your beauty before the midnight hour
Tells me it'll all be alright...

Before you came to me I travelled the long roads, I travelled overnight

Not an inch of earth left to scour
I never landed in any trouble I didn't invite
But your serenity before the midnight hour
Tells me it'll all be alright...

I'm lost for words, but there's no poet I can't recite
In my hand a stolen flower
Reminds me Heaven's far from sight
But your forgiveness before the midnight hour
Tells me it'll all be alright...

I knew our lives would be together woven
Like the plaits you wore as a little girl
Though but a boy, the heart had chosen
For you to look after mama's pearls ...

© Ed Fram 2020

23

My love

My love, she sleeps so softly
For me the night comes roughly
Like the wind singing tenderly to the sea
While it looks back, longing to be free

My love, her touch is gentle
My smile is just incidental
Her faith is all the stronger for it
Kneeling in hope is gone, so I just sit

I sit, waiting for her return
I sit, her parting words still burn
I sit, hanging by a thread
Clasping a lock from her head

My love, she's understanding
Never cruel or demanding
A friend in storm or fair weather
My love and I, always and forever

Forever, it's not long enough still
Forever, our love's cup unfilled
Forever, it can't warm this chill
I love you dear, I always will

My love, she sleeps so softly
For me the night comes roughly
Like the wind singing tenderly to the sea
While it looks back, longing to be free

© Ed Fram 2015

24

My midnight maiden

The naked stand so shameless
There's no cloaking their desires
The prisoners are all blameless
The devil doesn't stoke these fires

Warning wages a battle
Today we're on retreat
History's sabers rattle
Staving off tomorrow's defeat

Tear up your ticket before the midnight maiden
You wouldn't wanna leave a clue
I'll be on the last carriage at the end of the line then
Like I was only passing through

But every move's a mystery
No, I can't do it all again
I'd write you out of history
If only I could find my pen

Now the dawning hour's nearing
The light's wrestling darkness away
It's not as bad as you're fearing
Stop shaking like a bride's bouquet

The naked stand so shameless
There's no cloaking their desires
The prisoners are all blameless
The devil doesn't stoke these fires

© Ed Fram 2017

25

No place to wait

History cannot humble her, nor the echoing of hollowed
halls
Her serenity is fulfilled, when chaos and calamity calls
But what of these tears
As clear as the crystal above her gold-lined walls?
The future has been and gone
The bird's sung its first and last song
The nest's withered with no place to wait
As regret's rod is tired of looking for bait
And the sun, it always shows up too late
Yes, it always showed up too late ...

So who'd guess a bended knee
Could make me this happy?
But to keep it, who could know
You've just gotta let it go?
On the edge of things
See how the bird still sings
Though you and I know it's fate

As regret's rod is tired of looking for bait
And the sun, it always shows up too late
Yes, it always showed up too late ...

Do what you believe in
And believe in what you do
He believes in the unbelieving
And he believes in you too
So twist my arm, I'll force your hand
To the halfway house, at your command
To meet your demons and all their demands
Where you left them by the gate
Though regret's rod is tired of looking for bait
And the sun, it always shows up too late
Yes, it always showed up too late ...

© Ed Fram 2015

26

Northward bound

I'll give you all my years for just a few of yours
I'll fill them with riches, like the abbeys of those York-
shire Moors
And all the bells will sound.
Whitman's multitudes, Shakespeare's summer days
And all of Sinatra's selfish ways
They can barely begin to explain
How I found you lost in Spain, where streetwalkers com-
plain
There's not an officer in sight!
And the sailor, he has nothing new to bring forth
I'm with my gal and we're heading north ...

Don't meddle in the affairs of a rogue
No use asking the ship captain what's been stowed
Go to the docker, he'll soon tell you!
And what of the red girl, sent to sit between us?
I'll see to it that she's served well with a man who don't
spit and cuss

A careless mind seeking princely solicitude
Can always be found on the roof bathing nude
If you cared enough to look!
It's party time on fifth and fourth
I'm with my gal and we're heading north ...

A sharp tongue with a blunted mind
Just some of the wonders you can find
In the alleys of Hollywood
I'll take you far from that raging river to now
If the waters and their governing gods allow
We will speak softly of our lives to be
Your watery eyes are like diamonds to me
Let them rest near my shoulder
Most people spend their life just going back and forth
I'm with my gal and we're heading north ...

© Ed Fram 2020

27

O praise the King

A basket of wicker
See the flame flicker
With the Spirit's breath
Man no more left bereft
With faith in you I can't be failed
O praise the King, the Lord of Israel!

Laying low from upon high
Let all the world sigh
At the beauty of thy love
Let all proclaim thy grace from above
A name the angels can't cease to hail
O praise the King, the Lord of Israel!

Before my bondage I could see
Before I knew to ask to be free
You had saved me even then
You were the Word before the pen
On that cross sin was forever nailed

O praise the King, the Lord of Israel!

On rugged land we stumble on
Though broken voice, hear our song
Awaiting your peace at the very end
Longing to begin calling you friend
From the path I can't be derailed
O praise the King, the Lord of Israel!

© Ed Fram 2016

28

Only in dreams

Even now as my mind gathers dust
Golden thoughts of you could never rust
You had what I want but I got what you need
Days with dreams and routines still to feed

Like lovers and their silly schemes
We'll live on only in dreams
But it's always you that I'll miss
If you take nothing then please take this
It's always you that I'll miss
It's always you that I'll miss ...

You're so eager to know what's happenin'
You can change your shirt but not your skin
She ain't French but I like the way she kissed
Only it reminds me it's you that I miss

Like lovers and their silly schemes
We'll live on only in dreams

But it's always you that I'll miss
If you take nothing then please take this
It's always you that I'll miss
It's always you that I'll miss ...

So I'll just get high before too long
Or maybe I'll get drunk on our song
And I'll forget all the money I could earn
And I'll be learnin' to live or else live to learn

Like lovers and their silly schemes
We'll live on only in dreams
But it's always you that I'll miss
If you take nothing then please take this
It's always you that I'll miss
It's always you that I'll miss ...

29

Our love to live

Oh if my word
Could be that strong
To turn around
See how I went wrong

But it came too soon
From me to you
The winds of change
They're rushing through

My pockets are filled
Deep with grief
Plans so shallow
Our time is brief

The snow falls clean
Nowhere to hide
What does it mean
Without you by my side?

And if my song
Could still forgive
No hard so long
Our love to live

30

Painting in red

When your mind is with the sky and your heart's with
the floor
When your tears have travelled far and they can't roll on
no more
When you're painting in red, the night keeper comes to
your gate, she's leading you to the other door
You've seen it in nights long gone, you're sure you've
walked with Keira through this one before ...

To where they're chaining all the lame, there's just too
much hanging around
They're muffling all the ears, that ain't ever even sensed a
sound
And the chief's covering with spotty blindfolds, the eyes
of the blind
Then he'll be preaching about forgiveness to the forgiving and the kind ...
All the while floating free but framed in the sky above
him, a red object still so ill-defined

He'd tell you what it is, but then to the truth he'd always
be confined ...

When your mind is with the sky and your heart's with
the floor
When your tears have travelled far and they can't roll on
no more
When you're painting in red, the night keeper comes to
your gate, she's leading you to the other door
You've seen it in nights long gone, you're sure you've
walked with Keira through this one before ...

Now Keira has come to claim you, handing you a paper
trail with more keys to find
Saying it'll unlock all the other doors inside your mystery
mind
And the tuna tins are still falling all around you, from her
smoky sky
There's always plenty more fish in the sea she'll say,
when you try to reason why
But her keys just don't fit these cans
And they're hanging signs readin' Cezanne's
At all these door that still ain't yours to see
So as the master once did, you'll paint in red
The boy that you used to be
See you again tomorrow, he said
To be eternally captured and forever set free ...

So when your mind's with the sky and your heart's with
the floor

When your tears have travelled far and they can't roll on
no more
When you're still painting in red, Keira will come to
your gate, she's here to lead you to the last door
You've seen it in nights long gone, but this one you must
go through alone, never to know what for
And red is the colour you wore
Yes, red is the colour you wore ...

31

Pillow poems in deep blue

The pillow's poetry don't really sleep
As an angel looking for lost wings weeps
And like a spider trapped inside its own web
The post-modern man dreams of the old
He's a free spirit but does what he's told
To taste your touch don't make it true
The band's packed up and I'm still singing the blues ...

Somehow the smoke made things clearer
Each step away and the end seems nearer
As the clock moves in time with the clicking of crutches
These days, when paradise talks everyone just watches
But I breathed in the bay in the half-light
Wondering where time's tides had taken you
I know that face, it don't match the shoes
The band's packed up but I'm still singing the blues ...

So I figure money's got a lot to answer for
A cold heart melted by scorching sorrow
Oh how it always leaves you wanting more!
Here comes the doc and his bag of tricks for endless to-
morrows
The couch man asking what makes me tick, like he only
knows
But you don't choose the rain any more than it chooses
you
The band's packed up and I'm still singing the blues ...

The pillow's poetry don't really sleep
As an angel looking for lost wings weeps
And like a spider trapped inside its own web
The post-modern man dreams of the old
He's a free spirit but does what he's told
To taste your touch don't make it true
The band's packed up and I'm still singing the blues ...

© Ed Fram 2017

32

Roses of regret

When all you've read leads to a Godhead
you always fled
When the last tears have all been shed
Bled dry to see the children protected and well-fed
"Then you'll be a man my boy!" father always said
With that in mind, I now thee wed
Until we be dead
Yes, until we be dead ...

Wishing for health and wealth but getting malady and
hunger instead
Dreaming of better times laying here in bed
And painting the sky all the earth's colours except red
For red is the rose of regret you once said
Yes, red is for the rose of regret ...

The sun supervises the super-drying of the damned
Wild flowers still hold meaning for the land
Needing each other like a bolt needs its thunder

The squally rains are blowing us under
So take these roses of regret
Take them from me so I can forget
That tomorrow's a day we'll never get
Yes, tomorrow's a day we'll never get ...

© Ed Fram 2016

33

Second thoughts

What of the one you never took?
She sees further than you
But was just too afraid to look
How she cares for right and wrong
When your darkness was so long
What could have been might still be
If you embrace what it is to be free

So fruitlessly the sweat-soaked soil's unearthed
With nothing left, the barren boy's been turfed
From where the unnatural vines took root
End times a-nearin' with nothing left to shoot
So make the land pay, but it'll cost you the earth
Make the land pay, but it'll cost you the earth …

There's a chill in this bed, the romance is dead
The thrill's still, they danced at the funeral, I read
We didn't plan it well, we took it all just the way they fell

You always said the last to ring the bell will be the first to
hell

So fruitlessly the sweat-soaked soil's unearthed
With nothing left, the barren boy's been turfed
From where the unnatural vines took root
End times a-nearin' with nothing left to shoot
But this earth's too small a price to pay for a second birth
This earth's too small a price to pay for a second birth ...

© Ed Fram 2019

34

Singing in the rain

From long ago 'twas written, though it ain't yet been
taught
The right to say it true, a right for which the victors
fought
But knowing where they came from, with their history
hidden so well
The satisfied sky wept its tears of joyful misery and rang
its thunderous bell
Ringing for the deaf, not hearing their own screams
Weeping for the refugee, refusing to give up on dreams
Ringing for the downtrodden, rain-sodden
abandoned child of winter's unceasing war
Weeping for choirs of orphans, singing for families a-
feastin'
never tasting completeness at their own door
And the rain does pour
Yes, the rain does pour
Yes, the rain does pour ...

But long ago 'twas written, though it ain't yet been taught
The right to say it true, a right for which the victors
fought
But knowing where they came from, with their history
hidden so well
The satisfied sky wept its tears of joyful misery and rang
its thunderous bell
Ringing for the elders, ignored by the unknowing gener-
ation of peace
Weeping for the anguished, childless mother who can't
get no release
Ringing for the silenced and sacred, whose prayers go
unheard
Weeping for the vanishing wisdom of his long-awaited
word
And the rain will pour
Yes, the rain will pour
Yes, the rain will pour ...

For long ago 'twas written, though it ain't yet been
taught
The right to say it true, a right for which the victors
fought
But knowing where they came from, with their history
hidden so well
The satisfied sky wept its tears of joyful misery and rang
its thunderous bell
Ringing for the falsely slandered, whose name can never
be restored

Weeping for the innocent, incarcerated ones now facing
the swift sword
Ringing for the bells that can't be rung no more, with
their cut down rope 'n' cord
Weeping for the poor man, who knows a chewed-up
crumb is more than he can afford
But the rain must fall
Yes, the rain must fall
Yes, the rain must fall ...

© Ed Fram 2015

35

Smile for me

Write these words down for me
I don't own them anymore
It's gettin' too close to just let it be
Ain't clear what I'm searchin' for ...

Smile so sweet like you did before
When you don't see me no more
Just smile sweet like you did before ...

Take what's gone by from me
I ain't lookin' back no more
It's gettin' too dark to see
The ghosts are gatherin' at my door ...

Smile so sweet like you did before
When you don't see me no more
Just smile sweet like you did before ...

Lift this weight from off of me

I can't carry it no more
It's gettin' too heavy, set me free
I'm prayin' with my knees to the floor ...

Smile so sweet like you did before
When you don't see me no more
Just smile sweet like you did before ...

Smile your smile again for me
We can't laugh like we did before
The day is closin' with your beauty
How could I ever ask for any more?

Smile so sweet like you did before
When you don't see me no more
Just smile sweet like you did before ...

© Ed Fram 2015

36

Snowfall

"It's you, not me" so said the sign
Let's meet over coins and coffee
Like there's really something on the line
But how many amens will make amends
For the easy life that you're living?
Sliding across floors of sweat shops
Ignoring the children on train tops
All the while gloating about your giving
The good girl in skinny jeans is gone
Drawn to a man of means ain't wrong
But citing the greats don't make it so
She asked for sunshine, I got snow
Drowning in purity, the only way to go

"You ain't welcome here" the sign it surely spoke
After all I've done for you, is this some kinda joke?
Led by those you commissioned
Grappling with your own greatness
On the brink of ruins yet envisioned

Rendering Nicene nectar tasteless
Welcome to London, England
Land of crowns and broken crosses
Make sure the stations are manned
Count the victories not your losses
But citing the greats don't make it so
She asked for sunshine, I got snow
Drowning in purity, the only way to go

I looked at my futures
They numbered three
"It's you, not me" firstly
Near "You ain't welcome here"
And the snow fell clear
The snow fell clear
The snow fell clear

© Ed Fram 2016

37

Springs pass by my door

What can I say
When words have no meaning?
What can I do
To rid me of this feeling?

In love all is fair but 'tis fleeting
You always told me so
I knew it from our first meeting
Though now I really know
Sometimes there's only one basket
To pile your bounty up on high
But then again there's only one casket
Only one chance to touch the sky

Who will lend a hand
When I can't reach out no more?
Who will send me flowers

When springs pass by my door?

The desert dunes talk to the mountain moon
The sun waits for a place to call home
I'm working on the meaning of see you soon
Is that when the final bird has flown?
Half-past never has long ago come and gone
You ain't returned, so why drag it on and on?
Please there's no need to apologise, it's time to be realistic
now
I should've known it by how you speak and the way that
you bow ...

But what can I say
When words have no meaning?
What can I do
To rid me of this feeling?
And who will lend a hand
When I can't reach out no more?
Who will send me flowers
When springs pass by my door?

© Ed Fram 2015

38

Tales from Scheherazade

The thread's been drawn from the last loom
There's nothing left but the clown's costume
It's ready to soak up all of your lost tears
Now watch out for the gavel of the auctioneer!
Sad faces sell double-quick, ain't that clear?
But a million man hours
and a thousand tales from Scheherazade
Won't bring back a second
from that moment we never had ...

All the votes are in, they've all been accounted for
Apart from these spoiled ballots strewn across your floor
"A nod for the one who's committed no sin!"
The pens are being tested to find the ink it's written in
Do they belong to the last man laughing or the one with
the biggest grin?
But a million man hours

and a thousand tales from Scheherazade
Won't bring back a second
from that moment we never had ...

Follow the beggar back to where he first led
Beneath the arch where all the books remain unread
Look out there'll come a time he'll follow you!
But then he'll turn to toot you a too-da-loo
Don't you wish you'd listened closer, so you could go too?
And a million man hours
and a thousand tales from Scheherazade
Won't bring back a second
from that moment we never had ...

The armies of wheat have been gathered by the farmer's
feet
It ain't the season, but Arabella asks you for a trick or
treat
You're baffled, this ain't on the question sheet
And why is her smile lookin' so indiscreet?
"That'll be four guineas!" she smiles with conceit
And a million man hours
and a thousand tales from Scheherazade
Won't bring back a second
from that moment we never had ...

© Ed Fram 2015

39

Tears to call a friend

The also-ran
on a track with no bends
The rocket man
in a space that never ends
The suffering one
smiling playin' pretend
The lover
only tears to call a friend ...
The mother
without a lamb to tend
The sinner
to hell he'll descend
Unaware
of ways to ascend
Past the lover
with only tears to call a friend ...

Now the attorney
with no crime to defend

Leaves the judge
with no case to suspend
And the jury
no verdict, they'll resend
For the accused artist
without a landscape to mend
The poor one
a long dime left to spend
But the master
on him, he does depend
His servant
faithful to the end
And the lover
still only tears to call a friend ...

© Ed Fram 2015

40

The broken road

There's a song in every smile
In the fruit each tree brings
A song for every mile
On this road of broken things ...

There's a song for every bird
A bird for every song
Honey, you got my word
It was you all along

There's a song from long ago
Carried on angels' wings
A song for us to know
A gift for lovers to sing

There's a song in every smile
In the fruit each tree brings
A song for every mile
On this road of broken things ...

84 | ED FRAM

41

The shadow of a star

Together we'll dance,
alone we must mourn
Those that have died,
those never born.
You are all I am,
I am all you are
Let's light the path by candle,
or the shadow of a star.

The devil's not in the detail, it's in the way he walks.
So loosen the tongue twisted in idle talk,
for scheming, so rotten on the downtrodden.
In fields forever fallow, with the scent of flowers long
forgotten,
they'll bind you saying "love is the key to wedlock".
But in their suitor there's no piety to unfrock.
So turn your sail to the isle far away,
where you and I will some day lay ...

And together we'll dance,
alone we must mourn
Those that have died,
those never born.
You are all I am,
I am all you are
Let's light the path by candle,
or the shadow of a star.

For His robes we'll be picking cotton,
pure as the snowdrops of Hermon.
Praise Him, the only begotten, turn our ears for to hear
the sermon.
With sacred oil upon his beard and face,
He leads, to where peace and righteousness embrace;
where hatred and greed disappear without a trace,
far beyond the mountain road to the land of grace ...

Together we'll dance,
alone we must mourn
Those that have died,
those never born.
You are all I am,
I am all you are
Let's light the path by candle,
or the shadow of a star.

© Ed Fram 2020

42

These three words

What would I say to you
If we could speak no more?
How would I greet you
If you walked through my door?

Tell me, did you know you'd be gone so long?
Did you savour the sweetness of our last song?
Did the rain wash you clean like you did hope?
Did your skin grow thick to help you to cope?

And what would you say to me
If we could speak no more?
How would you greet me
If I walked through your door?

For I never thought you'd be gone so long
I never sung it like it'd be the last song
The rain came and went, the pain must remain
Skin a-thickened, for thinnin' memories to wane ...

Now what would I say to you
If we could speak no more?
Just three words to the one I adore
How would I greet you
If you walked through my door?
With three words to the one I adore ...

And what would you say to me
If we could speak no more?
These three words I pray,
but I can't say for sure ...
And how would you greet me
If I walked through your door?
With these three words I pray,
though who can know for sure ...

© Ed Fram 2015

43

To the ends of your smile

Lead the way laughing and I'll come following you
To the ends of your smile, as long you hand me a clue
For only the commander can taste the solitude of surren-
der
Only a watchmaker knows the time it'll take to mend her
And we will arrive where beauty beats the big idea
Where meaning is deepest, when it ain't understood so
clear ...

Lead the way laughing and I'll come following you
To the ends of your smile, as long as we're back by two
For only the widowed heart can sense the silence of sepa-
ration
Only the stage player can pretend he don't need no stand-
ing ovation
And we will arrive where beauty beats the big idea
Where love is strongest, when it ain't felt quite so near ...

Lead the way laughing and I'll come following you
To the ends of your smile, as long as you share my point
of view
For only the artist can know the captivity of creativity
Only the prisoner experiences the joys of being free
And we will arrive where beauty beats the big idea
Where gold is brightest, when it ain't held so dear ...

Lead the way laughing and I'll come following you
To the ends of your smile, any place away from here will
do
For only winter worries can dim the summer's sun
Only a speechless heart can tell me you're the one
And we will arrive where beauty beats the big idea
Where seasons are welcomed, without asking the time of
year ...

Lead the way laughing and I'll come following you
To the ends of your smile, I'll bring along the whole crew
For only a gathering of many can speak out against the
few
Only gates not yet dreamed, can keep us from getting
through
And we will arrive where beauty beats the big idea
Where the song is sweetest, when it ain't heard through
fear ...

© Ed Fram 2015

44

Veena's voice

A young man's eyes, an old man's tears
You've come far on silver sitar
You've come near on golden guitar
But you can't hide from unfound fears
You can't disguise the lost years ...

So send me a silver sitar
Grant me a golden guitar
And a flute to toot and any lute to shoot
But it'll never near Veena
Man, you shoulda seen 'er!
Yes, it'll never near Veena
Her voice still calls like a wistful sonatina

A young man's eyes, an old man's tears
You've come far on silver sitar
You've come near on golden guitar
But you can't hide from unfound fears
You can't disguise the lost years ...

And India ain't far from where my mind and time first
met
But regret still has an appetite to whet
Yes, regret still has an appetite to whet
So I'll feed it with these sad songs
The ones written by thickets of thornless thistle
The ones about that serene soundless whistle
And I'll tell all but I've kissed not one
And I'll stow it all away in carpetbags
And I'll tag 'em all "reminiscence's rags"

So send me a silver sitar
Grant me a golden guitar
And a flute to toot and any lute to shoot
But it'll never near Veena
Man, you shoulda seen 'er!
Yes, it'll never near Veena
Her voice still calls like a wistful sonatina

A young man's eyes, an old man's tears
You've come far on silver sitar
You've come near on golden guitar
But you can't hide from unfound fears
You can't disguise the lost years ...

And I'll sit and stare at them elephants on strings
They even come with a bell that rings
You said they're all things to all men
But you'd better think again

For it'll never near Veena
Man, you shoulda seen 'er!
Yes, it'll never near Veena
Her voice still calls like a wistful sonatina

Yes, her voice still calls to me
The voice with no choice but to be
And I've come far on silver sitar
I've come near on golden guitar
But I can't hide from unfound fears
I can't disguise the lost years ...

© Ed Fram 2015

45

Where the wind blows

Where the wind blows
That's where I'll be
You'll find me 'neath that fallen tree
Where the wind blows
It don't bother me
You caught my eye, you set me free

Where love lands
No man can tell
Who waves the wand, who casts the spell?
Where love lands
I do so wish you well
But who'll hold your hand, who'll ring the bell?

Where fate leads
I'll follow it there
Through cloudy skies, without a care
Where fate leads
It's only fair

That you be near, that you be there

How time passes
Without a trace
I miss your touch, I miss your face
How time passes
Into space
Beyond our reach, before we find our place

Where the wind blows
That's where I'll be
You'll find me 'neath that fallen tree
Where the wind blows
It don't bother me
You caught my eye, you set me free

© Ed Fram 2015

46

White lies

You wished the rain would wash all away
I prayed that it would make you stay
A hand held out too far for the holding
Secrets of an ancient kind now unfolding
But in all your bravado, I was so subsumed
I thought you a real beauty, despite the cheap perfume ...

Now I've heard all your different stories
There's no reputation to defame
You can't hide behind distant glories
White lies can't believe the colour they became ...

We watched the sun rise above all
Our shadows rescued by darkest nightfall
This truth of ours, we cannot unrobe
For the depths of the seas, nor the roundness of the globe
You always pretended not to want me around
But when I left, you could barely even frown ...

I've heard all your different stories
There's no reputation to defame
You can't hide behind distant glories
White lies can't believe the colour they became ...

47

With Rodriguez

Flowers left saluting the sun
Quicksand's still on the run
The all seeing are crawling blind
Through the marshes of your mind
And I'm with Rodriguez in the rain

Your bell struck by my heel
My heart broken by your hand
I've forgotten what it is to feel
Who needs a chair to make a stand?

Still wind frozen at the paupers' portico
Sooner or later you gotta let it go
Bathed in bone-dry death droughts
Clowns and clouds bawling their eyes out
And I'm with Rodriguez in the rain

Your bell struck by my heel
My heart broken by your hand

I've forgotten what it is to feel
Who needs a chair to make a stand?

© Ed Fram 2016

48

Young at last

If you knew the answer too
You'd keep it between
Me and you
Where true colours can be seen
Through and through
And there's no need for
Another clue
To a perfect love, without a flaw
Watching where the wind last blew
But not asking it for much more ...

As the sun kisses the sea goodnight
I know you'll be back to hold me tight
Our courses may never meet again
But friend, there is but one end
I'll catch your streaming tears
Though they may be many years
From where we now embrace
I hardly recognise that face

Distances unlock home truths
So I'll sing this song of our youth
I'll sing this song of our youth...

If you knew the answer too
You'd keep it between
Me and you
Where true colours can be seen
Through and through
And there's no need for
Another clue
To a perfect love, without a flaw
Watching where the wind last blew
But not asking it for much more ...

© Ed Fram 2019

49

(Section Two) A little while

Burning time, filling pockets with paper
Not enough to light up a smile
Fate tells you it's just you and her
At least for a little while
At least for a little while ...

Playing with wicked words
Never understanding the game
Repeating what you've heard
Without ever knowing her name

Burning time, filling pockets with paper
Not enough to light up a smile
Fate tells you it's just you and her
At least for a little while
At least for a little while ...

New ideas ain't backed by old money
They'll tell you it just ain't right
No it ain't right asking bees for honey
When the same sun shines on all in sight

Burning time, filling pockets with paper
Not enough to light up a smile
Fate tells you it's just you and her
At least for a little while
At least for a little while ...

© Ed Fram 2017

50

A love like ours

It's all old before it's really begun
Half the battle is knowing it can be won
When you're tired of fast cars
And those cheap cigars
Come place your hand in mine
And know darling, you'll be just fine
Don't waste your time wishing on stars
Nothing can take the place of a love like ours

The penny can't drop
When it's stuck beneath a shoe
Time won't stop
Just to let a deathbed through
I'll rest when I'm long gone
I'll lay down beside the rock you're on
Even kings with all their earthly powers
Know nothing can take the place of a love like ours

Get up, get out

Show 'em what you're all about
The best is always left unsaid
Don't forget to make the bed
And all the things you do, that I'll never understand
They sure make sense when I hold your hand
Even the land that forever flowers
Knows nothing can take the place of a love like ours

It's all old before it's really begun
Half the battle is knowing it can be won
When you're tired of fast cars
And those cheap cigars
Come place your hand in mine
And know darling, you'll be just fine
Don't waste your time wishing on stars
Nothing can take the place of a love like ours

© Ed Fram 2020

51

A man of means

Blood's thicker than water
A wad of cash is thicker than both
A mean man for your daughter
Or a man of means to betroth
The more I find out
the less I really know
What it's all about
And which way to go

Water for the body
Like truth for the soul
These new old clothes, so shoddy
Stained with the hatred they stole
The more I find out
the less I really know
What it's all about
And which way to go

But when the idea's this good

There ain't no waitin' around
Stories shared like they should
Their past's makin' up ground
The more I find out
the less I really know
What it's all about
And which way to go

So lawyer up the land
On the book, place a hand
But remember, where there's no will
There's a way, still
Yes, always a way, so still
The more I find out
the less I really know
What it's all about
And which way to go

They always did their best
Fillin' heads full o' dreamin'
And "you're better than the rest!"
Emptyin' pockets with their schemin'
You're believin', so why protest?
The more I find out
the less I really know
What it's all about
And which way to go

Blood's thicker than water
A wad of cash is thicker than both

A mean man for your daughter
Or a man of means to betroth
The more I find out
the less I really know
What it's all about
And which way to go

© Ed Fram 2016

52

A purple star

I've flown ten thousand miles
Alone in outer space
For a souvenir and a smile
To disappear without a trace
The pickings, they were rather small
A purple star, a mask without a face
I suppose it's another one for your wall
Where misery ain't out of place
Time changes everything
But nothing changes time
And so we'll sing
And the bells will chime

Sweet mama, the dawn breaks
Now who's gonna fix it?
Escaping by torch, all it takes
And the mind tricks it
To think you're seeing light
Through Chinese canvas cares

Go on, look all you might!
But it just ain't there
Time changes everything
But nothing changes time
And so we'll sing
And the bells will chime

Your voice echoes with no shame
You ain't really here
I'm still so glad you came
Still wanna draw you near
Though skies are all around
Our cries will not be heard
We never made a sound
They always had the last word
But time changes everything
Nothing changes time
And so we'll sing
And the bells will chime

© Ed Fram 2016

53

A rescued rose

I'm existing but this ain't living
When you've given everything worth giving
How much longer can you go on?
Even time'll turn against you before too long
So I'll see you at the crossroads
Where many a troubled mind unloads
To find an unburdened back still broken
Lips unsealed, the words left unspoken
Yet the sun set and rose, as it should
Our love never goes, as if it ever could ...

You made me your captive
so I'd be free to love again
Kindness can be deceptive
When you're caught out in the rain
But there's no land left for building
The warrior's sword's no more for wielding
Still blame doesn't know his name
Yes, blame cannot know his name ...

And the sun set and rose, as it should
Our love never goes, as if it ever could ...

And so and so, the years did flow
Through rock and winter's snow
Thin air is thicker than blood
A spring of hope, a rescued rose bud
From nothing we came
With a heart for hire
Our love all that will remain
But of this we will never tire
For the sun set and rose, as it should
Our love never goes, as if it ever could ...

© Ed Fram 2015

54

Acceptance in southern winters

Hear this story of love seeking acceptance in southern
winters
Like sin needing repentance from the cross that never
splinters
Amid the fruit of its liberty tree
Rooted in the rising anger of the free
But tell me, are you beautiful enough to be truly faceless?

Go find the brothers of sleep
Keep learning the ways of the dead
Follow the master like a sheep
And forget everything you've read

I washed my hands in your tears
If only I could now bring you near
Back to the place where it was told
That story of love, a love so old

See the sick rose withering
Like its art really matters
It's time to take stock, no dithering
This glass don't break, it shatters

Now hear this story of love seeking acceptance in south-
ern winters
Like sin needing repentance from the cross that never
splinters
Amid the fruit of its liberty tree
Rooted in the rising anger of the free
Then tell me, are you beautiful enough to be truly face-
less?

© Ed Fram 2017

55

Addolorata

Dirt paths lead us
From place to place
Laugh we must
But tears we'll taste

You can buy time
But you can't return it
I'm gonna make you mine
So you'd better earn it

Shadows fear the day
That night won't fall
Like when you went away
And took my all

Now's no time to talk
You wouldn't understand
Can't tell which way to walk
No one to hold my hand

When the dust settles
Come follow me
With precious metals
And a broken key

Confusion's for the weak
Only one way to be
Listen to them speak
Of longing to be free

Cloud or shine
It's all the same
We're doing just fine
You know my name

© Ed Fram 2016

56

Appian Way

Take your worshipping ways, go build yourself another
temple
There's no space for these feelings you've left within
I can't be chained to a mood and skin so simple
When I'm still the original orphan child of sin
So I'll meet you along the Appian Way
Though there's really no more left to say
The words were all long ago defined
Now all that's left are the tears of time

No man can tell which way to turn with a father's watch
a-gleamin'
Save for the son and his ragged army in wretched retreat
But who has seen further through your eyes forever
dreamin'
When I believe there's finally no one but loneliness to
greet?
So I'll meet you along the Appian Way
Though there's really no more left to say

The words were all long ago defined
All that's left are the tears of my mind

I've never known wealth, but riches I've had a-plenty
Carry me on this choir leading the way all soft
Drownin' the riotous as their barrels roll on empty
But we mustn't be seen, cut the carollin' motor off
And I'll meet you along the Appian Way
Though there's really no more left to say
The words were all long ago defined
Now all that's left are the tears of time ...

© Ed Fram 2015

57

Artless love

I am when you are not.
Here to tell all, all telling truths.
I was when you were not.
Here to sing farewell to our youth!

Your heartless art of blackened snow,
subjected to the sun's imperial shadow.
You always knew when to lay low,
and when it was another case
of artless love to go ...

A high priestess governing love for the rude and untaught,
sending the fish to their watery bed.
Their mouths agape, soon to be caught;
they should've known better, you said.

Guard your pocket well,
without memory or knowing of fate.
Watch your fortune swell,

soon the beggar will be at your gate!

Watch the young girl, how she dreams;
turning the hands of mother time.
She'll tell you what it all means;
how the world's worries ain't worth a dime!

I'm forever waiting for eternity.
But you're so reluctantly willing,
to pass it all off as modernity,
being so deathly and life-giving
In the way you are ...

I am when you are not.
Here to tell all, all telling truths.
I was when you were not.
Here to sing farewell to our youth!
© Ed Fram 2018

58

Ballad of a black bird

We came to see the view together
but I'll be fallin' off this edge alone
As black bird sits on the bench beside mine
And it's picked up my tossed stone
thinking it'll be the meal of all time ...

Just as the second hand pokes fun at the others
I'm lapping you time and time again my brothers
But the master's eyes always gaze at us first
To the minute and the hour, he'll look
We hold all the power, I read it in our baptismal book
The one that's not been out the drawer
Since 1964 ...

Yes, we came to see the view together
but I'll be fallin' off this edge alone
As black bird sits on the bench beside mine
And it's picked up my tossed stone
thinking it'll be the meal of all time ...

Look out for the sniper, he's readied his gun
But the enemy has already moved on
He's left aiming at the sun
But he always wanted to shoot for the moon
Now his bullet's gate-crashed the stars' party
And they're calling him to their feast
It killed nobody, we'll just bend it into a spoon
But first you better offer that bird the sign of peace ...

Yes, we came to see the view together
but I'll be fallin' off this edge alone
As black bird sits stony still,
on the bench that was once mine
It's now down to the skin and bone
Picked on by another
who's thinking he's found the meal of all time
So help me Mary, earth's Elysian Mother
For I've still got me this cliff to climb
Yes, I've still got me this cliff to climb ...

59

Barn dance day

To the brave the sea speaks softly, of all that's gone be-
fore
Only for the timid do its waves roar
But the girl sat in the field, only a lantern and darkness
for company
Content with a crumb, of riches she ain't got any
They say beggars can't be choosers
But choosers can't afford to beg
So she'll drink to poverty and jive on bow leg
Yet gold is ruinous in paucity and abundance
So this ain't the time for a barn dance
No, this ain't the time for a barn dance

To all the trusted tomb makers
Gather your travellin' papers
We're heading out for one last trip
Over there, quit chewing a cigar that ain't lit
I see why they say there's no use for a man like you
But tell me, how do I appear to you?

Like I've worn love in all its colours?
Like unsung, uprooted words without the music of oth-
ers?
Left to till the land that made my forebears landed
To accept now what God has handed
For tables don't turn, they simply break apart
Sure, you're clever but you ain't really that smart
Or else you'd know the lower the struggle, the higher the
climb
Yet you tell me, you're doing just fine

Now there are those sprung from learned stock
To them, the masses will flock
But bottled guilt can't be traded drop for drop
So protect your homes with rocks and stones
Find out who's owed and who owns
But remember, there's no cure for blood on snow
No use turning up the heat, hoping it'll go
You came to it softly, so softly you'll go

To the man of breeding
Put down what you're reading
It can't help you none now
Tell me, who'll put out this fire and how?
Your money's up in smoke with each toke
No joke, in the summer before the dark unfurls
Where naked emperors swap messages from their lost
worlds
You've got history in your eyes
When you smile, others hide

They know when it all blows up
They'll be left feeling down
Unprotected by their learnings in town
For who can make a living from the dead
With a tag on their leg and a price on their head?

As for me, I'm just another rootless rambler
With destiny, I'm a gambler
The true tumbleweed man
First to the scam
The insiders' insider
They say I've had others besides her
But when you're dying of thirst
Who'll listen to talk that water'll kill ya!
Just as some work for a living
To see some kill themselves working
While for others the gold comes handed down
From rags to rugs, to a house in town
But I know there's plenty of time to live when I'm dead
It was a good call after all, to be lying here instead ...

© Ed Fram 2016

60

Beauty on my mind

Follow the fog to where roses lie in naked slumber
Astride widows' graves lying under
On the brink of wonder
'Tween death and the Great Guarantor of life
With nothing but charm to bequeath a wife
And I got beauty on my mind
Seekin' you out, bound-blind

The road's bumpy,
I'm filled with doubt
You're fuelled by hope,
I need a way out
Steep's the slope
We need to climb
So let's tell each other,
we're havin' a good time

The jokerman's sellin' bread free from taste
Get your grapes from the lady in fine lace

But don't forget to sign, leavin' in such haste
People need to know where they really were
A face semi-opaque, so fake - it can't be her
But I got beauty on my mind
Seekin' you out, bound-blind

The road's bumpy,
I'm filled with doubt
You're fuelled by hope,
I need a way out
Steep's the slope
We need to climb
So let's tell each other,
we're havin' a good time

I've been moulded by milder hands
than yours
Hatred unbounded, red in tooth and claw
Still not one has neared to caress the core
Like the one still standing at my door
An ill-placed patron, that much I know for sure
But I got beauty on my mind
Seekin' you out, bound-blind

The road's bumpy,
I'm filled with doubt
You're fuelled by hope,
I need a way out
Steep's the slope
We need to climb

So let's tell each other,
we're havin' a good time

© Ed Fram 2016

61

Belonging to be

For the ne'er-do-well springs
Nothing but disdain
For waters destined for the drain
As they gather by candle shine
To blame the sea
For washing it all away
Some day they'll stop the seasons too
No one is ever ready for change
when the same will do ...
No one is ever ready for change
when the same will do ...

I came across a thousand doors
I tried each and every one
With their rusty hinges
All pointing at the sun
Release me, till all ties are gone ...
Release me, till all ties are gone ...

Things are not made of wood and stone
But words and sweat, blood and bone
Each with each, as the ghosts of nations groan
There's no use quarreling the quarried heart
It's hollowed out, hollowed out from the start
An old-fashioned destroyer of dialogue
Who needs conversations anyway
When the mind remembers so little?
Who needs conversations anyway
When the mind remembers so little?

I came across a thousand doors
I tried each and every one
With their rusty hinges
All pointing at the sun
Release me, till all ties are gone ...
Release me, till all ties are gone ...

When your star shines, it sparkles
Your light is my home
And I'll know that I belong
When your name is my own
I'll belong with the maker of poems
Amid past tomorrows
I'll belong with the maker of poems
Beyond shadowless sorrows
Living to live and belonging to be
As for you, are you longing for love
Are you longing for love like me?
As for you, are you longing for love

Are you longing for love like me?

I came across a thousand doors
I tried each and every one
With their rusty hinges
All pointing at the sun
Release me, till all ties are gone ...
Release me, till all ties are gone ...

© Ed Fram 2017

62

Birdsong

I got a parrot
Like a canary it sings
I got a parrot
Like a canary it sings
But it swears, it ain't seen a thing
Before we know to have a plan
for what's happenin'
We'll all be looking for the man
that would be king
We'll all be looking for the man
that would be king ...

And I'll cry at the stopping of your laughter
Laugh at the stopping of your cries
Do you believe in happy ever after?
Do you see hope in those eyes?

I got a parrot
Like a canary it sings

I got a parrot
Like a canary it sings
But it swears, it ain't seen a thing
And if I was here, I'd be there
Returning to kiss the ground I cursed
War and peace, both are fair
Just depends which you pick first

And I'll cry at the stopping of your laughter
Laugh at the stopping of your cries
Do you believe in happy ever after?
Is your truth held together with lies?

I got a parrot
Like a canary it sings
I got a parrot
Like a canary it sings
But it swears, it ain't seen a thing
No, that ain't him
His shoulders all on the level
With crook'd crown, he'll drown not swim
Clutching our depraved gavel

And I'll cry at the stopping of your laughter
Laugh at the stopping of your cries
Do you believe in happy ever after?
Do you believe love never dies?

© Ed Fram 2016

63

Caged by coincidence

"Take this, take this" he pleads
Handing you an amulet to relieve all pains
The beast doesn't follow, it leads
Where smoke screens hide ill-gotten gains
And there's no perception of how it all works
In days of dishonesty, he's among those that never shirk
But you ain't a loner, you just have no friends here to
bring along
So take comfort that the end is known, before dancing to
the last song
Yes, the end is known before dancing to the last song

You and I caged by coincidence
Furious at our fate
Conceding to love's insistence
Caring came too late
So let's make the best of it
Anyway we know how
Let's find some place to sit

While the farmer milks his cow
There ain't enough to feed the poor
He says the soil is much too rich
But tell me what it's all for
Who'll escape damnation's ditch?

Go ahead, express your wishes to unassuming minds
Speak now before it gets too late
Reach beyond where fault lies in all you find
And you'll fail to find fault beyond the gate
But flatter the centurion and his men four-score strong
For their truth will come out before too long
And our end will be known before dancing to the last
song
Yes, our end will be known before dancing to the last
song

© Ed Fram 2015

64

Catching fish

The best stand I ever took
was when I upped to leave her!
Unreeled and unhooked
Now I can take me a breather
Yes, I better take me another breather ...

Cigar to the lips, that great reliever
Clearing the smoky air from a mind
confused and clouded blind
But I ain't signing no dotted line
all dried up and resigned
No, I ain't signing no dotted line ...

The best stand I ever took
was when I upped to leave her!
Unreeled and unhooked
Now I can take me a breather
Yes, I better take me another breather ...

A breather so I can forward fast
past memories of summer strolls by Lake Geneva
The ones we thought would always last
Now forever fading with each puff
you'll never retrieve her
So I'll just take me a breather
Yes, I better take me another breather ...

And who knows what I could find
Inside the smoke rings now filling my mind
It's too soon to give up
But too late to keep on the look
So just give me another breather
To relive the best stand I ever took
When I upped and left, a caught fish
unhooked ...

© Ed Fram 2015

65

Chaos' creed

Justice is demanding its wages, the tempter's left hanging
from the feet
The punishing pendulum is swinging in time with his
last heart beats
He was roped into it, committed for a crime he was never
committed to
But Doctor Doom cut the cord of conscience before be-
ing called on to tell right from true!
And the usher, he's blameless he needs to have his fun
too
As he leads you to your seats, from where the scaffold-
ing's in view
The eyes are fixed, as though with gallant glue
The mind wonders, when it will next be you

Justice is demanding its wages, the tempter's left hanging
from the feet
Who will guard the gallows when salvation's armies are
in retreat?

The waves fear the seas, the babe no more suckles at the
breast
Who will you call on to swear blind, when there's no fur-
ther witness to attest?
The season of giving reason has been eclipsed by mourn-
ful moons
When you're dedicated to despair and death can't come
to soon
The eyes are fixed, as though with gallant glue
The mind wonders, when it will next be you ...

Justice is demanding its wages, the tempter's left hanging
from the feet
But how can a bitter bee ever make honey that tastes as
sweet?
The great charter's been signed, we're now under chaos'
creed
No, there's nothing for you to read when it's all been
agreed
The agents of change will let you know if the birds will
ever be freed
If the fields will ever bloom and if the farmer can scatter
his seed
And the eyes are still fixed, as though with gallant glue
The mind can't help to wonder, when it will next be you
...

66

Dance it all away

A silver spoon for a tongue slicker than the smoothest
silk
Gathering all around, a crowd of countrymen and others
of his ilk
His face sequestered from the sun, he's speaking on our
behalf
Saying if you can't cry, you oughta laugh
And if you can't laugh, you oughta cry
Somehow, some day we all gotta die
But don't go asking me the reason why

Just dance, dance, dance it all away
Come what may
Come what may
Come what may
For time is short and the list is getting tall
Yes, time is short and the list is now so tall

You must surely see what brought us here

(Love and fear) can be hard to tell apart
Lifetimes wasted, what's another year
Trailing an upturned golden cart?
It's what you don't say, that really says it all
Turn your pedantic prose into a play
Throw out the script, let's have a ball!

Let's dance, dance, dance it all away
Come what may
Come what may
Come what may
For time is short and the list is getting tall
Yes, time is short and the list is now so tall

To the fatherless and hopeless, you stood in loco parentis
With the intelligentsia asking how it could end like this
For their ideas and ideals are chewed on now, spat out
and worse
And for the unknown brave soldier, only a beat up barrel
for a hearse
No flowers here, no wreath where upon a bed of bullets
he now lies
But you must keep on, this road won't walk itself, live it
through his eyes

And dance, dance, dance it all away
Come what may
Come what may
Come what may
For time is short and the list is getting tall

Yes, time is short and the list is now so tall

67

Dawn clouds fall

You're too busy to be happy
Trying to outrun destiny
You're chasing your own glory
It ain't yours, just set it free

The dawn clouds fall, it's hard to see
The sun is out, but it ain't for me
I thought we'd make it if we tried
The cursed chains can't be defied

You're too busy to be happy
Trying to outrun destiny
You're chasing your own glory
It ain't yours, just set it free

Lost leaves a-crisp, they're turning in
Seasons skip past tides we're travellin'
Your crystal face, your turquoise eyes
Lord knows, they can't be denied

Still you're too busy to be happy
Trying to outrun destiny
You're chasing your own glory
It ain't yours, just set it free

The cause is greater than the reason why
Can't you see I could never be that guy?
Flickers need coaxing to light up the sky
The stars never lined up for you and I

For you're too busy to be happy
Trying to outrun destiny
You're chasing your own glory
It ain't yours, just set it free

© Ed Fram 2015

68

Fair-weather foe

Born the wrong side of the river
Wagons circle, the coyotes quiver
The moon's pushed away like a swivel mirror
To bring the darkness that bit nearer
A desert-dry dungeon for a wishing well
Constantly overhead the pealing knell
Here Death is always the last friend to go
For the sailors of the sand and snow
He ain't no fair-weather foe
No, no, he ain't no fair-weather foe ...

One by one they be asking, before the trial is done:
Does your gold watch tell a different time?
Do your eyes see something hidden from mine?
There's more wisdom at park benches
Than from where this courthouse hands down sentences
To broken men just for asking "is this really all there is"?
And Death is always the last friend to go
For the sailors of the sand and snow

He ain't no fair-weather foe
No, no, he ain't no fair-weather foe ...

Darlin' when my number has come and gone
Don't be grieving none, just remember me in this song
With all those brave enough to hear it
And the good folk of the land will raise their hand, they
won't quit
Till the river be lifted
But Death will be the last friend to go
For the sailors of the sand and snow
He ain't no fair-weather foe
No, no, he ain't no fair-weather foe ...

© Ed Fram 2020

69

For Florence

You're the closest thing to perfection I'll ever hold
Brighter than a thousand stars and more precious than gold
Carry my love into your dreams
To make your darkness, day
I'll carry your dreams too, my love
As to the Lord we pray
"Hear us now, hear us loud
And carry us all the way."
All the way into your loving arms
Till the dawn of the last day ...

You're the closest thing to perfection I'll ever hold
Every gaze reminds me there's no wrong in you to scold
Carry my love into your dreams
To make your darkness, day
I'll carry your dreams too, my love
As to the Lord we pray
"Hear us now, hear us loud
And carry us all the way."

All the way into your loving arms
Till the dawn of the last day ...

You're the closest thing to perfection I'll ever hold
Lord keep you in your youth, though I grow evermore old
Carry my love into your dreams
To make your darkness, day
I'll carry your dreams too, my love
As to the Lord we pray
"Hear us now, hear us loud
And carry us all the way."
All the way into your loving arms
Till the dawn of the last day ...

You're the closest thing to perfection I'll ever hold
Remember me my sweet child, flourish in what you were
told
Carry my love into your dreams
To make your darkness, day
I'll carry your dreams too, my love
As to the Lord we pray
"Hear us now, hear us loud
And carry us all the way."
All the way into your loving arms
Till the dawn of the last day ...

© Ed Fram 2020

70

Free

He told me
Stand your ground, remember to keep your counsel
Needing gold don't make her no distressed damsel
Let your feet take you where they want to go
Let your mind tell you what you need to know
Then you're free
Yeah you're free

Singing the praises of his unrecognized genius
He's here but he's not really with us
A new season's coming round
But I still ain't found, no I still ain't found
Nothing but the same old school blues
Let your feet take you where they want to go
Let your mind tell you what you need to know
Then you're free
Yeah you're free

He told me

You gotta lose your mind to find your dreams
He said don't be defined by what it all means
Let your feet take you where they want to go
Let your mind tell you what you need to know
Then you're free
Yeah you're free

© Ed Fram 2017

71

Fruits of recompense

Your tongue's too tight to talk, but they've heard your
living voice
So the deal still ain't done, you've been given a final
choice
Your heart is asking them if it will ever be enough
Their sheep eyes fall silent, they're just so hard to bluff!

But she'll be there to greet you, the artist with the rainbow back
She'll ride you round the bend, always taking the inside
track
You'll know her from that ragged carpe diem cropped
shirt
She'll wash it all tomorrow, to be cleaned from today's
dirt

Your tongue's too tight to talk, but they've heard your
living voice

So the deal still ain't done, you've been given a final
choice
Your heart is asking them if it will ever be enough
Their sheep eyes fall silent, they're just so hard to bluff!

Go past the unknown swirling trees, from wild woods of
bygone times
They'll be handing out fruits of recompense, for all their
concealed crimes
And toying with the wind, they'll sound out their breezy
blues
But like Eve always said, you'll still have to choose ...

Your tongue's too tight to talk, but they've heard your
living voice
So the deal still ain't done, you've been given a final
choice
Your heart is asking them if it will ever be enough
Their sheep eyes fall silent, they're just so hard to bluff!

© Ed Fram 2015

72

Golden lyre of Ur

At times you look up, look out and question your lot
But money behind your parent's door
Kills ambition faster than an arsenic shot
So be careful what you wish for
And be thankful for what you don't got
Keep dreaming of that golden lyre of Ur
Bring back the balmy ballads our ears never forgot
Pluck each string raw and let your soul's sound
pour and pour out some more
Till our cups are overflowing, no tot
And with it, a new life we draw ...
Yes, you're the great king of lyres
and yet the true truth teller
You're no phoney sound seller
So guide my unyielding hands
Though unworthy,
Place them on your soft golden strands
And together,
We'll outsound a million bands

With this balmy ballad
And like sonic soldiers their hairs will stand!
See crying colours covering faces - no longer pallid!
See the bourgeoisie and boastful banned from your land!
And once more with your lyrical lyre, make life valid!
Pour out your musical majesty and restore
your kingdom as it once spanned
From corner to corner
Grander than grand
As it was always planned ...

73

Graveyard groove

A song in space
A dance in the dark
What use a car to race
With no place to park
As slogans shout out
Death to capitalism!
A post-romantic collectivism
With corporates on a cross
The poet at a loss
playing with words
For sentences never served
his time well

Now the drunkard
clutching a can, as he fell
More sorrows than solutions
But we wish him well
Knowing life will see The Thinker
Cut down to size

You can see it in his laughless eyes
Written out of history
In pencil

A southerly swinging in the trees
The rich do as they please
Never pausing to ponder
Lest they take leave of living
The wronged forced into forgiving
The abandoned still seeking their King
Captive to the capricious
With their unrelenting streams of hate
But they'll cease to flow before the date
Where scarlet girls are known to wait
Like dusts of desire in the air
For those going here and those going nowhere

But this boy never cared what he read
Even less to him what was said
Sensing that between the lines
We're all dancing on dimes
So work the wounds
The words will follow
Lie softly, lie softly
Every man's grave is hollow
Yes, every man's grave is hollow

One by her bravery
One ending slavery
One within a day

One without pay
One through what he reads
One turns his back on greed
One by the fountain new
One making many from few
But where is the one you're needing?

One through her hunger
One in silence yonder
One to never fear
One holding all dear
One to drink the cup
One to pull us up
One to lead the way
One holds still as the branches sway
But where is the one you're needing?

One with the lightest touch
One by keeping watch
One made to suffer slow
One gives without a show
One through faithful fortitude
One embracing sacred solitude
One with his great giving
One dying for a living
But where is the one you're needing?

74

Hearts of stone

The dead you've left can never follow you, no matter
how you smile
But eternity will surely be over after a little while
Yes, I'm sure I felt you walking beside me under the tow-
ering carved cross
Yes, I'm sure I felt you feeling the same loss
By that spot is written "he used to be..."
But to me, you're more than just a memory

Fire up another one under the boatyard's caressing cover
Each drag takes me closer to what's left for me to dis-
cover
But first it'll take away any life I've got left
This lighter that made you breathless and me bereft
Keep clutching this deathly dagger
Covered golden, it's lending me your old swagger
But when it stabbed you in the back
Why did you turn to me to apologise?
Is it because you had an accomplice, but no alibis?

The dead you've left can never follow you, no matter
how you smile
But eternity will surely be over after a little while
Yes, I'm sure I felt you walking beside me under the tow-
ering carved cross
Yes, I'm sure I felt you feeling the same loss
By that spot is written "he used to be..."
But to me, you're more than just a memory

Tuck your thumb away, there are no more full hands to
play
The corrupt croupier will be back to deal another day
Am I writing the words that you're now reading?
Are you filling your cup, while I lie here bleeding
With a dog for a pillow on the Queen's promenade
And a pram with all the possessions from my youth cru-
sade?
You're facing the crowd's bumbling applause
While the Roman soldiers all around me draw straws ...

The dead you've left can never follow you, no matter
how you smile
But eternity will surely be over after a little while
Yes, I'm sure I felt you walking beside me under the tow-
ering carved cross
Yes, I'm sure I felt you feeling the same loss
By that spot is written "he used to be..."
But to me, you're more than just a memory

You say the best things in life are free
But in death the best only comes
if you're prepared to lose your dignity
And the lightest things are dusty dreams
And the loudest are damnation screams
And the brightest are darker still
And the longest are unending days to fill
And the hardest are hearts of stone
And the worst is being all alone
Yes, the worst is being all alone ...

The dead you've left can never follow you, no matter
how you smile
But eternity will surely be over after a little while
Yes, I'm sure I felt you walking beside me under the tow-
ering carved cross
Yes, I'm sure I felt you feeling the same loss
By that spot is written "he used to be..."
But to me, you're more than just a memory

© Ed Fram 2015

75

Heathen heights of Hades

"Come with me"
Into the vade mecum
I'll take them
Into my treasured torture tome
Cover etched with skull and bone
Their name finds a home
Now they'll forever be kept with me
Under lock and key
Inside the heathen heights of Hades

Gold to make them groan
Through her
his diabolical deeds he honed
For the Devil don't work alone
He ain't no sole trader
So with furtive fetters he made her
do as he please

Now no chance of release
All in a day's work outside the
Heathen heights of Hades

For her the watchtowers are looming
All around black roses blooming
Beyond, acrid fumes pluming
Now see the gargoyles' ghoulish glare
Their tangled trumpets blare
To the tune of this frightful fanfare
For newcomers to greet
To his satanic seat
Inside the heathen heights of Hades

Now find the suited, booted kingpin
Always a grin
but he ain't no clown
With slight nod of head
The iron rod crashes down
His enemies dead
But no crystal chalice for him now
Just cupped hand
For his anaesthetic to land
Just a sip
For his sin-filled eyes to kip
And drift between gatherings
Of herb movers and Sheiks
Inside the gates
Of the heathen heights of Hades

Together their souls lie flat on belly aches
No food to be found amidst yellow lakes
A melancholic moan from those placed prone
A collective gramophone of grief
beyond all belief
Normal sounds from the grounds
That surround the heathen heights of Hades

Others found spine supine
'neath the soaring satanic skies
But resting this way or that
Arms raised or flat
All guarded over by the King of Lies
Any wrongdoing he denies
Inside the heathen heights of Hades

Cerebus, chewing on a shoe
is there watching over them too
Extinguishing all love, hope and faith
in the doomed dirt pit
His eternal remit
One head for each of those ought to do
But there's plenty of backup here too
Everyone's got a job to do
inside the heathen heights of Hades

All souls bought with His blood
To be ageless heavenly angels
Now their pain tells
Of the error of their ways

Looking on the One they betray
And together they say
"Send us a second Son please!
Save us from the heathen heights of Hades!"

"No can do, He was the only One
He was sent to warn
But you chose to adorn
with scorn and Jerusalem thorn
So now you're reborn
As babies of Hades
No ifs, buts or maybes
Your souls' sacred shelters are torn
For your loss the saints do mourn
And with Tartarus' triumph
your part of paradise does perish
A place a true believer would cherish"
His words echo, slow
A parting blow
for those inside
the heathen heights of Hades

And one by one
We didn't heed the call
As paradise vanishes for us all
Into a demonic daze
All our souls ablaze
And all that's left are the
Heathen heights of Hades

76

High road underground

Where's all the hope gone?
Only dark where your light once shone
The reaper's here, gathering what I sow
In the place where dreams go to lie low
I've lost count of the stars you left for me
Oh baby bring back your love to me

Where do I begin, where do you end?
Blurry-eyed lines 'tween ocean and sky
So let's play pretend
Deaf to those asking why
I've lost count of the stars you left for me
Oh baby bring back your love to me

Straight talking, crooked walking
On the path of our making
It's the high road underground I'll be taking

The silence of repentance the only sound found
Shaking the ground, where I last had you
I've lost count of the stars you left for me
Oh baby bring back your love to me

© Ed Fram 2016

77

HMS Lost at Love

The merchant ship unloads at the dock
As the pendulum on karma's clock
Patiently waits to swing back from whence it came
As you change the vessel's name to match the false claim
That you were really lost at sea
That you ever really did love me ...

A loaded question disguises more than loaded dice
Like how once you asked, why didn't you think twice
Before taking us to the hall
Where all the seats are standing?
Kicked to the corner at the ball
Trying to meet all you're demanding

But I ain't breaking the law
I'm only living outside it
I'm on the first ship-to-shore
Before the destination's been decided
Sailing on, come fair wind or storm

As the sun sinks beyond the deck
Never to rise to greet eyes so forlorn
Call in the divers, it's just another wreck

Rates ain't of interest without a dime to invest
The police make another arrest
An innocent man has failed their test
Revealing only their true colours
While free is the crime lord, protected by your dirty dol-
lars
So I wear steel bracelets and you're in fur collars

The merchant ship unloads at the dock
As the pendulum on karma's clock
Patiently waits to swing back from whence it came
As you change the vessel's name to match the false claim
That you were really lost at sea
That you ever really did love me ...

© Ed Fram 2017

78

Hollow hearts

When your best only takes you halfway up the hill
And the rivers have run their last
What's the sense in rushing, there's time to kill
And existence has come and passed
But where do we go from here?
When you just say hello dear
Like we never been apart
And jealousy's just an empty feeling
Hollowing out your heart

The girl said she could read my mind
Though I never did care for signs
She asked me to spare some change
Guess I can't be spared if I stay the same
But no, please don't thank me none
Just did what any other fella woulda done
Now where do we go from here?
When you still say hello dear
Like we never been apart

And jealousy's just an empty feeling
Hollowing out your heart

Be there my friend, stay a little while
With me to the end, to the last long mile
For there ain't no mountain we can't move
No stone too big or small
When there's nothing left to prove
That's when you'll hear them call
But where do we go from here?
When you just say hello dear
Like we never been apart
And jealousy's just an empty feeling
Hollowing out your heart

They're calling for the nameless one
The one without a face
They're calling after memories
Of all who came from that place
Covering their face for fear
Hiding in shadows of shame
So I'll just say hello dear
like we never been apart
For jealousy's just an empty feeling
Hollowing out my heart

© Ed Fram 2016

79

I dreamed I dreamed

I dreamed I dreamed
Of daisy-kissed feet
When the lights go out
And there's no one but you to meet

I dreamed I dreamed
Of perfect dreamy nights
Where no morn can break
And there's no one but you in my sight

I dreamed I dreamed
Of boundless things
Where seasons stand still
And the sunless silence to your eyes that it brings

I dreamed I dreamed
Of lovers who can't be saved
Where the sea waves tribute
To us and all the rivers it gave

So I dreamed I dreamed
Of daisy-kissed feet
When the lights go out
And there's no one but you to meet

© Ed Fram 2020

80

I turned

I turned my eyes to the top of the hill
where a lonely flag did stand
I turned my ears to the wind but it blew so still
As I stood where the sea meets the sand
I turned my dreams towards His will
then headed for the land

I turned my hand to toil the land
But dust and stone did it return
I turned on my heel for one last stand
To bone and skin with nothing learned
I turned my fears to your command
Now there's no need for any concern

I turned to reach all the truths
As pearls for the pigs below
I turned towards the steps of my youth
Eternity has time to kill, that I much know
I turned to silence the streams of my heart

Let us forever grow but never apart

I turned to wait at the sea of snow
Aside trains with no place to go
I turned to the peaks of the Pyrenees
Their beauty will have you on your knees
I turned to say goodbye to the graces of the Lord
And all the joys we could never afford

I turned and turned to stumble on stones
Desolation deep to the marrow of bones
I turned away though You did call
Ignoring starry nights that make you feel small
I turned to silence the streams of my heart
Let us forever love like it was the start

© Ed Fram 2018

81

I'm your man

Outside the birds are calling
Like I'm calling out to you
While autumn leaves are falling
Like I'm falling into you
Break a window, unhinge that door
Gather up a bit of the floor
We ain't coming back here no more

Take what you can
Honey, leave the rest
Pretend I'm your man
Like I passed your test

Dusty books speak of tomorrow
Shiny ones talk of what's been and done
Why buy what you can borrow?
The uniform ain't here to police our fun

Take what you can

Honey, leave the rest
Pretend I'm your man
Like I passed your test

Outside the birds are calling
Like I'm calling out to you
While autumn leaves are falling
Like I'm falling into you
Break a window, unhinge that door
Gather up a bit of the floor
We ain't coming back here no more

© Ed Fram 2016

82

Journey man

Wherever you're going, I'll be travelling along
So long as there's room for two
But darling, I ain't gonna write you a song
Just to prove there's nothing between me and you ...

You say you got all the guilt
And none of the glory
But no unnecessary blood was spilt
In the making of your story

The gas needle's showing nil
But you've got time to kill
"Honesty pays!"
I hear the thief say
As he pockets my watch

And the colour of that guy's skin
Don't mean he should be comfortable in the job he's in
But honey you'd be so far gone

If we started talking about them rights and wrongs

Wherever you're going, I'll be travelling along
So long as there's room for two
But darling, I ain't gonna write you a song
Just to prove there's nothing between me and you …

© Ed Fram 2020

83

Knocking at your door

Every picture tells a story
If you let 'em, some will tell you even more
Houses ain't for living in
But to see who comes knocking at your door

Does the bud reason when it is the season
For its flower to bloom?
Should the one in torn clothes not question those in
princely robes
Who never put hand to loom?

But mamma said be careful living on a shoestring
You'll tie yourself in knots
It don't matter if you don't know a thing
It's all about what you got

So clothed in money to feed the flesh
No crucified carpenter, no chance to start afresh
Scorn for a poor soul, it starves

Still, with His blood He carves
With His blood He carves, so still ...

Hail Caesar's centurion, a cross he creates
Thinking it a craft of his own making
To ash and dust, Sin the carpenter cremates
His lifeblood turned to His deathbed

Every picture tells a story
If you let 'em, some will tell you even more
Houses ain't for living in
But to see who comes knocking at your door

© Ed Fram 2017

84

Lead me all the way home

Heal me with your truth, O Lord!
I'm so tired and so full of sin
Heal me, let me rest assured
That I'll be gathered safely in
Forever beyond the fold
A stray one all alone
Take me young, take me old
Lead me all the way home

He tells it straight,
His words like an arrow they fly
To pierce every shield of hate,
His truth don't lie
A truth that won't bend to wicked ways
A truth unchanged, no matter who pays

Take me over cliffs and haunted hills

Beneath me, only barren land
Past many a disused mill
Above screaming sea and silent sand
Past many a love laid to rest
Under bridges running east and west
Take me to where your truth is my own
Lead me all the way home

He tells it straight,
His words like an arrow they fly
To pierce every shield of hate,
His truth don't lie
A truth that won't bend to wicked ways
A truth unchanged, no matter who pays

The warm hand gives tenderly
What's been yours from the start
The cold one grants grudgingly
Only as it waves to depart
So feed me generosity, not gold
To give freely what can't be sold
And let the bells ring out from Jerusalem to Rome
Let the bells ring out and lead me all the way home

© Ed Fram 2020

85

Letters from a father

A washed-up crab-covered carcass
"Death by dangerous company"
Wild winds with hell's flames to harness
Carry letters from a father that ain't for me ...

We didn't quite cross paths
You could almost call it fate
In love at the same time
But on different dates

Open each door
We ain't got nothing to hide
There's nothing in the cellar
Not a thing inside
Save for rats and river water
And sailors' dreams of better tides

Where does the rain go
When it's tired of being teary-eyed?

Does the river still chase the sea
When all its waters have dried?

A washed-up crab-covered carcass
"Death by dangerous company"
Wild winds with hell's flames to harness
Carry letters from a father that ain't for me ...

© Ed Fram 2017

86

Long on fear

Lend me your eyes so I can see
Why you'd wanna be with me
'Cos from where I'm lookin'
Seems like nothin' but trouble's cookin'
In my kitchen and in my hall
Nothin' but lone talkin' at the wall
Now tell me, where do we go from here?
The wheels are off, ain't no point to steer
We're short on days and long on fear ...

Lend me your cares so I can learn to really feel
What it's like to walk with love as your Achilles' heel
'Cos from where I'm standin'
The heart that I'm a-handin'
Is heavy as stone and twice as hard
Smooth on the outside, internally scarred
So tell me, where do we go from here?
The wheels are off, ain't no point to steer
We're short on days and long on fear ...

Lend me your ears so I can hear
The hauntin' hums of those you hold dear
'Cos from where I'm listenin'
I sense only ripples of streams a-glistenin'
Not the rips of waves crashin' to the shore
Not the screams of loved ones at your door
So tell me, where do we go from here?
The wheels are off, ain't no point to steer
We're short on days and long on fear ...

Lend me your thoughts so I can know
What's really real and what's just a show
'Cos from this stage set
It seems you're treatin' me like we just met
And though memories must some day return to dust
It ain't right to cover our truth in the dirt of mistrust
So tell me, where do we go from here?
The wheels are off, ain't no point to steer
We're still short on days but long on fear ...

© Ed Fram 2015

87

Love at the maids' museum

I've learned from this good earth
the only thing worth
loving is love
I've come to know
the only one that'll save you from laying low is up above
So love, love, love ...

The face feeds as the soul starves
You see it whole, I only get halves
Look to the left, look to the right
But don't forget what's not in sight

The rich man tells all of the pain of plenty
Says it's greater than when you're running on empty
He prays at an altar of his own design
No stomach for the job but he won't resign

The cash goes in and up goes the chin
We play the same game, but only some can win
The soldier salutes solitude, claims it's better than being
alone
Says it's all about attitude, as he fires to declare his demil-
itarized zone

My baby, she's proud to have a panhandle named for her
At the maids' museum
The old masters line up in the depths of winter
Just so they can see 'em
And I've been searching for words to rhyme eternally
But I've never beaten the simple beauty of you and me
No, I've never beaten the simple beauty of you and me ...

© Ed Fram 2017

88

Madly in love

Madly in love, we left sanity with hate
Minds weighed down, too much to contemplate
I see you in me, a reflection run free
On closer inspection, I see only me
No one will love you
No one like me
When you ain't even looking
It's amazing what you'll see

It's been said many times, no more words to add
It started out so good, so good it was bad
How can a perfect pair be so odd?
One a velvet glove, the other an iron rod
No one will love you
No one like me
When you ain't even looking
It's amazing what you'll see

When only darkness remains inside

At my lowest ebb, in you I'll confide
If stars could see their own dying light
Would they need to burn so bright?
Would we let them out of our sight?
No one will love you
No one like me
When you ain't even looking
It's amazing what you'll see

© Ed Fram 2015

89

Magic and honey

They'll ruminate with Rumi
Placing Plath on a plinth
Looking to sue me
For hiding their soul in a labyrinth
They consume pretty verse by the minute
But never rehearse to see what's in it
Lest they should ever really understand
The pain of an unborn baby howling in the rain
Blackening the electric sky with its cry
Daring to hear the answer to why
But ain't it funny
Life didn't turn magic and honey
Like you thought
Was it worth it
All those battles you fought?

Beyond the pulpit of profit
Far above the reach of dragons and ravens
No human shields, no safe havens

To eclipse the escapism of time
Where bells are frozen mid-chime
Where sin has no memory and no master
Yes, beyond the empty coffin
Beneath the earth, unearthed and hollow
Rise suns and silhouettes of swirling swallows
Each pretending that tomorrow never happened
Now ain't it funny
Life didn't turn magic and honey
Like you thought
Was it worth it
All those battles you fought?

© Ed Fram 2016

90

Mercury majesty

Don't believe the eyes your father gave you
Nor the lies of a mother torn in two
But take this stone from off my chest
For you're stronger than all the rest
Yes, you're stronger than all the rest
Please take it from off my head my dear
Out of sight, out of mind, any place not here
And then we'll see the summit and submit
To its mercury majesty and all that's within it

Yes, we'll see the summit and submit
To its mercury majesty and all that's within it
Don't question the feelings I give to you
Nor if the prayers of the saints are true
How can there be anything left to profess
When you were so much wiser than the rest?
Yes, you're still so much wiser than the rest
But time has has no master, save for the clockmaker
If they promise you eternal love, watch out they're fakers

And together we'll see the summit and submit
To its mercury majesty and all that's within it

Yes, together we'll see the summit and submit
To its mercury majesty and all that's within it
Don't doubt the truth I give to you
Nor if the waves of the sea are blue
And who but the sinner must confess
That you were always purer than the rest?
Yes, you're still so much purer than the rest
But knowledge knows nothing until before him it lies
unashamedly naked
Stripped of its hypocrisy with all falsity shattered and no
more held sacred
Only then can we see the summit and submit
To its mercury majesty and all that's within it
Yes, only then will we see the summit and submit
To its mercury majesty and all that's within it ...

© Ed Fram 2015

91

Missing memoirs

Those missing memoirs, they never seem far
Their words have gone to wherever you are
For there is but one author
Though our stories differ
For we all have a choice
We're all born with a voice
Some choose to silence others
Some choose to act as brothers
But missing memoirs will never seem far
Their words have gone to wherever you are

Now I'm wiser in my ignorance, seeking the father I
never knew
Ignoring the wisdom of princes, who follow others for a
clue
Like a slave with no master
Like questions with no answer
Left to dance merry with the fool
And challenge life to a death duel

But I'm wiser in my ignorance, seeking the father I never
knew
Ignoring the wisdom of princes, who follow others for a
clue

There's beauty in all I see
I ain't no saint but I'm down on my knees
When weary for worthless wealth
You came to me by stealth
A bolt from beyond the blue
I'd seen, but I never really knew
Now there's beauty in all I see
I ain't no saint but I'm down on my knees

Those missing memoirs, they never seem far
Their words have gone to wherever you are
For there is but one author
Though our stories differ
For we all have a choice
We're all born with a voice
Some choose to silence others
Some choose to act as brothers
But missing memoirs will never seem far
Their words have gone to wherever you are

© Ed Fram 2016

92

Monday's sin

Time like the lady's lullaby is singing itself softly back to
sleep
The old man in the frame is weeping as he now speaks
To you he's been gone for years, but to him it's only been
a week
Now blazer boy boasts his words are final, there's nothing to add to his critique
But which side will you be on when the show comes to a
close?
And why does Monday's sin always feels worse in Sun-
day's clothes?

We're just the same you and me, we share the same air I
believe!
The Duchess of Duke Street is gasping she'd rather die
than breathe
Victory and defeat are arguing, it ain't clear whose face
should be the first to show

While canine clouds howl around the night watchman,
who's demanding all must know
But which side will you be on when the show comes to a
close?
And why does Monday's sin always feels worse in Sun-
day's clothes?

Your ghost carries a shovel, he can't wait to bury you
Your waving is wayward, you'd better give him another
clue
Now hope and damnation, they're having one last dance
They're eating out of his hands, the juggler's got them in
a trance
But which side will you be on when the show comes to a
close?
And why does Monday's sin always feels worse in Sun-
day's clothes?

© Ed Fram 2015

93

Musandam moons

My delicate dreams drift
On midnight's Musandam moons
And evening's stiff tiff
Has passed too soon ...

So play me that music, my Musandam muse
Lead me to the eternal King of Ormus
Singing still, in the Sea of Fars
Singing still, no matter where you are

And rouse me from my slothful slumber
Drag me bleary-eyed and under
But keep closed the eyes of the unknowing
And together we'll keep going
With my ears filled to the brim
Carried on your Hormuzian harp hymns

Play me that music, my Musandam muse
Lead me to the eternal King of Ormus

Singing still, in the Sea of Fars
Singing still, no matter where you are

For my delicate dreams drift
On midnight's Musandam moons
And evening's stiff tiff
Has passed too soon ...

© Ed Fram 2015

94

No ice please

A full moon's better than none at all
A tear for each time you call
Like the coster, a filled cart on an empty street
The concierge with no one to greet
The unbeliever needing God more than he could know
There's nothing like hard luck to soften the blow
But I needed love, more love than you could show

You said I sold my soul
When I was buying back my heart
The meek look pitiful, that's their role
Another charity for the rich to start
But they never look the same way twice
So roll on, roll up and roll that dice
Another martini, this time no ice ...

Where were you the day the authorities took the blame
For not treating all the different colours the same?
They're saying no more "right place at the wrong time"

But it's not justice when you still got me waiting in line
Others skip on past
Here, the last really is last

You said I sold my soul
When I was buying back my heart
The meek look pitiful, that's their role
Another charity for the rich to start
But they never look the same way twice
So roll on, roll up and roll that dice
Another martini, this time no ice ...

© Ed Fram 2016

95

Noonday moonbeams

Ah! But there's nothing new under the sun
And there's no greater truth than saying you are the one

...

You say there ain't no smoke without fire
And if I told you it was steam
You'd call me a liar
But things ain't what they seem
Around here, eternity itself is set expire

And there's nothing new under the sun
And there's no greater truth than saying you are the one

...

We'll sit here stranded puffing noonday moonbeams
And pen poems of drowning dawns yet to transpire
But we're only mirroring the upwelling waters of life's
back-flowing streams

And while you're still dreaming of dreams that could inspire
Just remember:

There's nothing new under the sun
And there's no greater truth than saying you are the one
...

© Ed Fram 2015

96

Nothing but this song

I wait, I wait for the rain clouds to go sailing by
Resolved to burn the near-blackened clocks
I can't ever let go of your lily hand, I won't even try
For my teardrops there's no space at the docks

I never knew where I did belong
Some have a lineage long enough to hang from
Still unmet hopes weigh down my feet
Leaving me to chant alone, throwing shadows at the
street

Of her silken scarf, she cannot be dethroned
Who dares unpluck the precious flowers in her head
As the morning breeze low moans
My eyes will ache from the tears they shed

The sword's truth shall never be dulled, its steel will
never surrender
From tongue to tongue her story shall be told

From Chaucer to The Old Pretender
More life in her, though in linen she be rolled
And I have nothing but this song to send her ...

© Ed Fram 2020

97

Of heads bare and crowned

How much is it to get a reaction these days?
Love is free, but it sure makes you pay
Measure for measure, to the penny
Days of plenty, I ain't seen many
So I'll wait till it's as good as it was bad
Remember me by what I did, not what I had
With one eye to see what the other just knows
Struggling to pursue a myth, forgetting how the story
goes

Be careful what you wish away
You might need it some day
Holding a mouthful of hurt with no bite
No, there ain't a tooth in sight
Amongst the few, of heads bare and crowned
And those that never wanted you around
And those who use power most nobly

And those who love humanity
But hate feeling human

Who knows how it feels to see a father fail?
Watching the innocent poor, who can't make bail
But the war ain't over, it just ain't started yet
Some day I'll write out all the words on a string, without
regret
To see if I can get back to where we started
To meet with the golden ones and the newly departed

Be careful what you wish away
You might need it some day
Holding a mouthful of hurt with no bite
No, there ain't a tooth in sight
Amongst the few, of heads bare and crowned
And those that never wanted you around
And those who use power most nobly
And those who love humanity
But hate feeling human

A Madame to the rich, a miser to the poor that never
flatters
When all is said and done, all that's left is all that really
matters
You're hosting a party you never wanted to attend
Your deeds are well known, why play pretend?
For it ain't how far you run, but high how you jump, my
dear
So no man can rise above you, ain't it clear?

Be careful what you wish away
You might need it some day
Holding a mouthful of hurt with no bite
No, there ain't a tooth in sight
Amongst the few, of heads bare and crowned
And those that never wanted you around
And those who use power most nobly
And those who love humanity
But hate feeling human

So quit telling me, show me instead
Was it ever real or tales told me in bed?
You distracted with your beauty
Then slayed me with your charm
I never missed the call to duty
I never meant to bring you any harm
Now I'm left wondering if fish ever get thirsty
With all the time in the world, why be hasty?

Be careful what you wish away
You might need it some day
Holding a mouthful of hurt with no bite
No, there ain't a tooth in sight
Amongst the few, of heads bare and crowned
And those that never wanted you around
And those who use power most nobly
And those who love humanity
But hate feeling human

Tell me, why this curse upon my shoulder?
No need to toughen me up, I can't grow any older
Tell me, how did I ever do you wrong?
No, I was never made to be this strong
You didn't wait for the times
You made them instead
The freedom bell chimes
As I lay down my head

Be careful what you wish away
You might need it some day
Holding a mouthful of hurt with no bite
No, there ain't a tooth in sight
Amongst the few, of heads bare and crowned
And those that never wanted you around
And those who use power most nobly
And those who love humanity
But hate feeling human

© Ed Fram 2015

98

Orphan X

Your words wither without water
The sun scorches the silhouette
Your eyes are in your daughter
To see you, though we never met
Did I get the face all wrong?
Didn't you guide me all along?
Our turn at life imitating art
But tell me, where do circles start?

Too long, too far and too fair
Have those arms been to me
Memories now thinner than air
Yet real enough to see
Orphan X never asks why
Wiping soot from the effigy of her ex-mother
Overhead coal fills the sky
And she's dreaming she's the child of another ...

Mamma's holding the gun

At the temple of coincidence
With razor-sharp tongue
And a blunted conscience
To cut you up and cut you off
From what could have been
But justice won't take no payoff
Ain't no part of her sordid scheme

Too long, too far and too fair
Have those arms been to me
Memories now thinner than air
Yet real enough to see
Orphan X never asks why
Wiping soot from the effigy of her ex-mother
Overhead coal fills the sky
And she's dreaming she's the child of another ...

© Ed Fram 2016

99

Our point of no return

My ghost, strung out on guitar
Strung up on a hill not far
There's no sense going back
To our point of no return
Pass me the candle and a bottle from the rack
I've got all your letters to burn

Winter's a drag, worse than tobacco smoke
If the wind don't get you, the air will sure make you choke
There's no sense going back
To our point of no return
Please don't unpack
Where you go, ain't my concern

For us, the sun must set, the moon will wane
And only this song will remain
There's no sense going back
To our point of no return
Blame it on the lost lilac

Go find another to spurn

Seek out another footman to reprimand
For honey, I was never at your command
There's no sense going back
To our point of no return
I can't just give what you lack
It's something you've got to earn

My soul, it sings out in the heavenly choir
Raising hell to avoid the eternal fire
There's no sense going back
To our point of no return
There's nothing left for us to bury or bring back
The next pilgrims are waiting in turn ...

© Ed Fram 2020

100

Sands of time

Even an arm of Herculean acclaim
Can't hold back the smallest grain
In life's sand clock
So inside time's cell, we'll remain under key and lock
And time's tune will ceaselessly play on
Tick-tock, tick-tock, tick-tock ...

But what if we reverse the sands of time?
Grab the glass and press rewind
Surely it will then sound a different chime
One that'll get us out of this nick
One that'll see the clock's lock picked
Tock-tick, tock-tick, tock-tick

But it seems we can't just choose and pick
Which events to erase and those we'd like to stick
For our past is engrained in each grain
Once through, forever altered
So first time round, don't falter

For time's tune will always be the same
Regardless which way round passes the grain
And for meddling, its sands are gonna run double quick!
Tick-tick, tick-tick, tick-tick

And soon the glass will shatter
In all directions, sands will scatter
To be washed up to shore
Building blocks for the little ones you adore
But their castles won't stand tall
If the sands don't speak to them of your fall
And stuck between little toes
Where they've been, what they've seen
They'll never know
Unless they listen close and soon
To time's ceaseless tune ...

© Ed Fram 2015

101

Second is first

I'll be travelling back to Epirus alone
'Though a victor's parade, I'll surely be shown
I've been struck by that old winner's curse
It's come along and emptied my purse
And sometimes it seems second is first

That morning, she turned to me and said
Whilst rearranging the bed
"anything you desire dear, I'm all yours, à la carte"
But you never told me that from the start
And all I ever fought for, was your heart
Now you're offering me culinary art
But I never wanted a plate of Picasso
It seems I've won the battle and lost the war
Now staring at your victor's menu, so hollow
Wondering what it was all for
Wondering what else could follow ...

And I'll be travelling back to Epirus alone

'Though a victor's parade, I'll surely be shown
I've been struck by that old winner's curse
It's come along and emptied my purse
And sometimes it seems second is first
"But you know it's warmer in your shade than in the sun
And right by your side, out of you a warrior I made
And all those battles that for me, you won
I was there as your soldiering shadow even when the
light had strayed
It was real for me too, it weren't no dry run
And yes, with your heart you've paid
But I wanted your soul, when all is said and done
But I still love you, hun
I love, I loathe you, I live you
I am you ..."

And I'll be travelling back to Epirus alone
'Though a victor's parade, I'll surely be shown
I've been struck by that old winner's curse
It's come along and emptied my purse
And sometimes it seems second is first

© Ed Fram 2015

102

Self-portrait blues

The poet, he's waiting for his review
Befriending those who like him the least
He has no view if his stuff's really new
Or if it's just never been released
But he sings about history too
Like it's never really ceased
Saying here nothing could be original
Except the rising of each sun!
And nothing's really unthinkable
Except that you might not be the one

Tell me, did you ever earn
This land that they're giving?
And when will you learn
About working for a living?
You say the poor ain't no concern
Long as the rich are forgiving
But it ain't your bridges that burn
It ain't my nightmare you're reliving

The fairest child in your mother's eyes
Born too soon for feeding
Hope fades with dusk, the soul never dies
Skies turn red, now I'm bleeding
When will I hear again, tell me sweet lies
It's your touch that I'm needing
But you'll need more than a mask to disguise
Every false move you got me reading
If you're trying to confuse our lows and highs
Honey, you ain't succeeding ...

The poet, he's waiting for his review
Befriending those who like him the least
He has no view if his stuff's really new
Or if it's just never been released
But he sings about history too
Like it's never really ceased
Saying here nothing could be original
Except the rising of each sun!
And nothing's really unthinkable
Except that you might not be the one

© Ed Fram 2017

103

Seraphim's song

With Seraphim's floating flames, the gardens of the sea
are never left unguarded
But who will cover us with angel silk showls after her
coals are doused and discarded?
How much longer will she burn bright with nothing to
reclaim but our blame?
We're rowing back on ourselves, yes I'm sure that house
is the same
See the captain signal to shore once more, he's saying
there's just no other way
But who will bring us aboard their land, when we're
drained of blood for pay?
And the sequin board is still telling all, he was with us
under a false name
So who can release me from this travellin' jail I'm in, but
my sweet Seraphim?
She can't tell a lie, but who will believe her saying it
wasn't really him?

The sky is crowned with compass clouds, it ain't clear
which way to go
It seems to me there's but a cracked pot at the end of this
rainbow
But now it's too late for those drawn in by his swagger
They must wait patiently while he slowly draws out a
dagger
Teasing and tormenting, but ever careful that the killing
is done just right
To please the baron, who counts tomorrow's eggs before
they're even in sight
And the sequin board is still telling all, he was with us
under a false name
So who can release me from this travellin' jail I'm in, but
my sweet Seraphim?
She can't tell a lie, but who will believe her saying it
wasn't really him?

The fame flourished and faded in that sour season, but
false fortunes still remain
A coin of gold for each grain of sand was handed, how
could it ever wane?
But the skin of the seed can never grow just the same
The train and track have been parted, like storm clouds
left without the rain
And who is there to blame when you're bone dry but
drenched in shame?
Bargaining with ghosts over what you wouldn't give to
glimpse sweet Seraphim again!

And the sequin board is still telling all, he was with us
under a false name
What can release me from my soul's cell but a dream of
serene Seraphim?
She can't tell a lie, but no man believed her saying it
wasn't really him ...

© Ed Fram 2015

104

Siberian sunsets

I hiked a ride with my thumb pointing down
So she took me back downtown
Where nothing looked the same as when I left
She later wrote a note blaming me for her death
There ain't a word these judges won't twist
I ain't no fighter, I can't make a living with my fist
But sometimes that's just how it goes
Good men laid low, Lord knows
That's just how it goes …

Some can't imagine a world in which they don't exist
But you never showed me reason to resist
The urge to leave here in haste
Some come with plus ones
Wanting to be seen from outer space
Some go minus egos
Too meek to seek their true place
From now, I'll follow the righteous road
From here to where the Tiber once flowed

I'll follow the righteous road …

You can't even call in on me from time to time
There's no crossing these lines
From the east out to the west
And those Siberian sunsets you liked best
It's all fading from your view
And know that I'll be passing through
Where the good men are so few
I'll be passing through and through …

© Ed Fram 2020

105

So long Susan

I saw eternal candles in your eyes
Now they flicker, it blows, it dies
To see a world filled with hope
Ruined by hate, I can't cope
Left only a chill to still the wind
At the window, where we sinned
Now the gate ain't ours to walk through
That touch, a farewell kiss, who knew
Forever would last so long?
So long Susan, so long ...

I poured out my sorrow story, my heart
All to you, word for word
You read not a letter, never made a start
To you, it was absurd
That I should be feeling the pain
Of you storming out in the rain
Having gathered the clouds above us
But now's not time to make a fuss

So long Susan, so long ...

I wish you only good
Like I know you would
If you were passing this way too
But what good is it to you
To pretend it never happened?
Not everything has a happy end
No, the gate ain't ours to walk through
This touch, a farewell kiss, who knew
Forever would last so long?
So long Susan, so long ...

© Ed Fram 2017

106

Some place downstream

The little men with big ideas
Chasing silver dreams
Downstream
From where we met, path clears
To a shallow hole
deep within, full of fleeting glances
So I'll swallow it whole
And retrace steps of first dances

Tears don't know which way to go
My heart beats just for show
So many ways to say I tried
Only ever one goodbye
A sweet note for reference
"The change made no difference"
Pain came and it'll go
Leaving me human

How many days pass between
each sunrise, seen through your eyes?
With tortured tangles of a man
Making funny angles as only you can
Out of the straightest of lines
And the death rod strikes its chime
But ain't it hard to turn on a light
in the dark?

Bouncing shadows across broken bars
Full winter moons come in jaded jars
So tired of the cold they're in
But you're still seeking solid silver spoons
What's left has been sold, better get going
Leaving only memories in the mirror
Of all those nameless faces
and faceless names
That time won't remember

© Ed Fram 2016

107

Song yet sung

You'd better leave in the direction of travel my friend
Get out of here before the tracks start to bend
Like the river you been mirror talking to
And when she comes to you without her clothes of cap-
tivity
Will you speak with a broad pen or will you show her
real pity?

So sing out your song yet sung
Defy the reacher's rules
Someday we'll all be one
The labourer will down his tools

There'll be times from time to time, just standin' at a loss
But patience is your vocation and eternity's your boss
Yes, a dangerous method for conquering the chaos
So smooth the blind corners of circumstance
With sincerity as your alibi at the last dance

Sing out your song yet sung
Defy the reacher's rules
Someday we'll all be one
The labourer will down his tools

Fill the time in between on your marching powder
Silence the love of blood with a voice that cries louder
Please, Mister Postman you're in plain sight now, can we
just meet?
Will you bring the vintage postcards of the house on car-
nival street?
I'd like to draw comfort but thinking about it only makes
it worse
So here's to bringing life to life and killing the dead with
a hearse

Sing out your song yet sung
Defy the reacher's rules
Someday we'll all be one
The labourer will down his tools

Pick up your portable alters of golden, laden with fine but
fickle pendants
The court has been readied, but where's the chief defen-
dant?
The judge says you'll do, we're all Abraham's descendants
But when harmony's attained, will you show me how to
fly?
To be a high church triumphantly declaring the story will
never die

And sing out your song yet sung
Defy the reacher's rules
Someday we'll all be one
The labourer will down his tools

© Ed Fram 2015

108

Soselo's song

Soselo's song still
With its youthful yodel
in children's ears rings
Concealing the stings
That blistered and burned
Each enemy in turn

For even the devil likes to dance
But don't give him no second glance
For you ain't gambling fleeting gold
This truth so often lies unopened, untold
It's our souls unsold he's buying
With a song so sweet, he'll keep trying
and his music, so mystic
even the pacifist turns militaristic
and with its Luciferian lyrical leaps
even the illiterate and deaf it defeats

But you hold firm to the end, my child

Resolute against the wicked and wild
Until Soselo's song no longer rings
in our children's ears
Teach them the torment it brings
And let them never forget it, in all their years ...

109

Source of sorrow

I turned my back on the human race
Man's just a lower form to chase
So I'll follow the storm to a calmer place
Content with ideas for friends
For we can't be rescued from our dead ends
And this ain't no stage to play pretend
With words yet unspoken
Treasures to save, never to open

But tell me, what do you see
What do you see, so clear?
Is it really me you want lying here?
And when your dreams hide in fear
Is it still me you want so near?
Words beyond the grave remain unspoken
A treasure to save, never to open

And amid the trees, I just can't fail
See how the wind whispers our tale

From long ago, they've seen it all
Stories told before loose leaves fall
Yet these words remain unspoken
A treasure to save, never to open

The river, it carries on carrying on
No matter what else is going on
To streams, they've never been so strong
But mama, she's been wrong all along
And these words remain unspoken
A treasure to save, never to open

You left the clock ticking down
A final say before leaving town
And this water's clean enough to drink, but too clean for
to drown
Yes, it's clean enough to drink, but too clean for to
drown
So what's beyond the grave will remain unspoken
A treasure to save, never to open ...

© Ed Fram 2016

110

Standby seducer

You keep me like a star to shine bright
Just another one of your standby lights
Once your sky's ready to be turned on
Then you think I'll disappear
as though I never once shone
But I'm still standing, I'm still here
I'll hit the headlines before hitting the road
On rivers of gold, to undreamed lands of old
Inside a canvas so clean it could've snowed

I've heard it all before
Yet somehow still want more
Your lies sound so good
They must be truthful!
You did it just 'cos you could
I swallowed it by the bucketful
But like an onion with layers to peel
You gotta fight the tears to reveal
A core that still knows how to feel

While all around is a-hardened
And the executioner, with raised axe
He's forever begging your pardon ...

All the toil for oil and coal
Won't make up for the words you stole
Like a second son, who knows he is the one
That will never truly be tested
But now that you've come and had your fun
Your mind can never again be fully rested
And if you hear of my despair, have no fear
It's only hot air, gone from here
To fan the flames beneath you

I've heard it all before
Yet somehow still want more
Your lies sound so good
They must be truthful!
You did it just 'cos you could
I swallowed it by the bucketful
But like an onion with layers to peel
You gotta fight the tears to reveal
A core that still knows how to feel
While all around is a-hardened
And the executioner, with raised axe
He's forever begging your pardon ...

© Ed Fram 2017

111

Star sign solo

We shared blurring bodies
At the emergence of time
We both used to be somebody's
But I still think you're mine
For you, love's another hobby
I'm stuck looking for a sign ...

A bored man's I love you
In foot-high neon glow
Well babe, I love you too
It's a shame you had to go

Take your final penny, it's earned its pride of place
Lay it above the fire, beside his beaming face
Pitch it against the raging sun
Now all's been said and done
Wage it on the winning horse
Now the race has been won

But pay the piper fair
His cares ain't his own
All that he declares
Is true, it's been shown

How we shared blurring bodies
At the emergence of time
We both used to be somebody's
But I still think you're mine
For you, love's another hobby
But I'm still looking for a sign ...

© Ed Fram 2017

112

Sugar hit

Keep it simple, stay sweet
Keep it simple, stay sweet
Your smile's a treat
Can't go without it
I need my sugar hit
I need my sugar hit

The poems came free
They poured outta me
Now I can't buy me a line
Not for a nickel, not for a dime

Close the door
We've heard it all before
Close the door
We'll let you in when we want more

Move on, you're free
Shake your head at me

Take a cab and just be
You ain't needed, you'll see

Keep it simple, stay sweet
Keep it simple, stay sweet
Your smile's a treat
Can't go without it
I need my sugar hit
I need my sugar hit

© Ed Fram 2017

113

Sweetest of wine

With your touch so fine
You turn my sour grapes
To the sweetest of wine
And I never committed no crime
But you took my heart, you took my shoes
And you walked me straight outta my blues

With your touch so fine
You turn my sour grapes
To the sweetest of wine
And I never committed no crime
Never even looked at the face of a dime
That weren't mine
So how come I got me the steal of all time?

With your touch so fine
You turn my sour grapes
To the sweetest of wine
And I never committed no crime

And what did you get outta me?
Nothing but sorrow and misery
But I guess that's all now history

And with your touch so fine
You turn my sour grapes
To the sweetest of wine
And I never committed no crime
But before we sip it, let's raise a toast
To the Father, Son and Holy Ghost
Giving thanks for bringing you to me
Though it all just remains a mystery

And with your touch so fine
You turn my sour grapes
To the sweetest of wine
Enough to last us till the end of time ...

© Ed Fram 2015

114

The choirs of Saint Paul's

These days the more I listen, the less I really hear
But who could ignore the calls to hear the King here?
Who could ever quieten the choirs of Saint Paul's?
Who could ever quieten the choirs of Saint Paul's?

Now which way do I go, an unhooked kite within that
unbounded sky?
Slayed and swayed on the breaths of temptation, where
death goes to die
Excuse their appearance while our ghosts meet the rising
sun into the wild
Though your arms be tied firm, open your heart, embrace her child
For this ain't no easy place to rule for the returning king
No pity for piety with nothing to hear, as the saintly eagle
sings

These days the more I listen, the less I really hear
But who could ignore the calls to hear the King here?
Who could ever quieten the choirs of Saint Paul's?
Who could ever quieten the choirs of Saint Paul's?

And the father, he's been outlived, now what more is
there for me to do?
The jester says better laugh at yourself, before laughing at
me too
He's planning for the big day,
as he rips out your eyes
Still expecting apologies to come his way
See on both sides of the Jordan in disguise
Here wait the dukes and poets stranded but jolly
Stooping unknowingly beyond their own folly
Gathering poems and fragments, their delight on the Isle
of Devils
Where the phasian bird circles to manipulate nothing-
ness on other levels

And these days the more I listen, the less I really hear
But who could ignore the calls to hear the King here?
Who could ever quieten the choirs of Saint Paul's?
Who could ever quieten the choirs of Saint Paul's?

But you could at least let me know, it's just common
courtesy
As you line-up for your morning hit of unreality, most
carelessly

Amidst the void of war in the land of jade writings of
conscience and politics fade
Ceaselessly lording over the outing and bettering the best
The original Venus with her mirrors, so much brighter
than the rest
Above sprawling sacrifices on shot-up foreign beaches
I can only write out their names in sands no man reaches

And these days the more I listen, the less I really hear
But who could ignore the calls to hear the King here?
Who could ever quieten the choirs of Saint Paul's?
Who could ever quieten the choirs of Saint Paul's?

© Ed Fram 2015

115

The house of harm

Hear the wide-eyed sailor
He's telling of a beauty not yet known
Listen as he speaks so softly
of elements pure but never shown
He tells of drowning in the waters
that protect and defend you
When the waves have lost their charm
Of when your fortress has flowed against you
Bringing danger to mourning mothers
and daggers from the house of harm
So look at me now and tell me what do you really see?
The same love and affection or just some kinda apathy?

Hear the warble of the warrior
He's calling the tribes to arms
As we drift away silently
Sailing on seas so calm
A tear for every occasion
Beyond the house of harm

Bitterness and tragedy, I found plenty of it with you
Solace in solitude and the meaning of existence too
And life's empty promises
Somehow they're leaving me fulfilled
If we can't go with the flow
Tell me who else will?
And who would bet against you
Holding all the aces as you do?
You made me the accomplice
The crime was finding love in you
Others nonchalant and novice
You left them without a clue
Ripped both asunder, no promise
While I found my love in you

And I'll hear the warble of the warrior
He's calling the tribes to arms
As we drift away silently
Sailing on seas so calm
A tear for every occasion
Beyond the house of harm

The crazy, creative type, he's left all alone
With a kiss so warm and gentle
Imagination must claim him as his own
As the three ravens return to the oriental
From whence they've once flown
But the night, it belongs to us at last
So take the red rope, reel us in to shore

The laughter must die down
The clown will cry some more
And the sails will soon slacken
Promise you'll never let go
The skies will surely blacken
I promise I'll never let go
There ain't nothing natural about nature
Only a game of cat and mouse
The reaper's always out to getcha
Only harm comes from his house

And I'll hear the warble of the warrior
He's calling the tribes to arms
As we drift away silently
Sailing on seas so calm
A tear for every occasion
Beyond the house of harm

© Ed Fram 2015

116

The idea of now

He hides behind the broadest sheets, to disguise his nar-
row mind
The land is handed over, the deed's been named and
signed
The glass shatters around us, the monocle man has
turned all highbrow
And the elders and bright young things are all left to
wonder exactly how
So bring in the choir master, search out the pink spotted
cow
But how much longer will he stand alone reasoning with
the idea of now?

For the promised change to come, you'd better bet on
Betty's yard remedies
She's gathering dead flowers and marketing happiness
with melancholia's melodies
So when you brush shoulders with your unwed wife,
you'll know you should've done more

The stretched truth will collapse to avoid paying tax, the
answers are all written on the floor
Across the delta, waves are descending on the confused
temples of Macau
But how much longer will he stand alone
reasoning with the idea of now?

Don't obstruct the carriage doors, whether you're leaning
out or leaning in
Others read Italian stories of succeeding sacred knights
while travellin'
What I can see of your face looks pretty enough, as you
hold your nose all lofty to the sky
I shoulda known there and then, attitude always follows
the footsteps of heels so high
And the ambassador smiles at his freedom flag, it's nailed
to the wall so still
I'm in the driver's seat now, chewing on Cleopatra'a poison pill
The ancient saints and latter day sinners are coming together, there's still a field to plough
But how much longer will he stand alone
reasoning with the idea of now?

© Ed Fram 2015

117

The law of love

I gaze into the night sky,
I look out from mountain tops by day,
The beauty of your work,
compels me to fall to my knees and pray.

From the baptism of first light,
shining down on the earth's face,
the law of love was written inside each heart,
and the stars were fixed in place.

Unmoved by shifting sands,
there to guide the way from the start,
some day the earth will vanish without a trace,
but the law of love will remain inside each heart.

The Son sent with a light so bright,
the rebel of the night may see the folly of their way,
with the law of love now written in His own blood,
we know the part each must play.

Lord, hear my humble voice,
though it be but a tremble,
fill my lungs with blessed breath,
so that your flock may assemble.

All will gaze into the night sky,
looking out from mountain tops by day,
and the beauty of your work,
compels all to fall to their knees and pray.

© Ed Fram 2020

118

The little girl circles

Walk the river
With moon and misery for company
I'll be on the other side
The other side, my honey
But you were always so good
at avoiding unwanted attention
You feared fame would give you purpose or at least it
could
Taking you back to the start of some kind of circular per-
fection
The kind you've been trying to escape so long
Where the little girl circles, as the lone lover plays on
Where the little girl circles, as the lone lover plays on

Walk the river
With moon and misery for company
I'll be on the other side
The other side, my honey
With the priest, his scales weighing your every word

Working out if they make sense enough to be heard
Or if they are plainly too absurd for repeating
The bride will see you now
Take to your seats and bow
The formality is only fleeting
And the little girl circles, as the lone lover plays on
Yes, the little girl circles and the lone lover plays on

Walk the river
With moon and misery for company
I'll be on the other side
The other side, my honey
Where the vultures pick up the scraps
From the table at love's last meal
I gave it my all hun, I had your back
But don't worry none, it ain't a big deal
So sweep the steps, clean as you go
Who knows when the mayor might show
Where the little girl circles, as the lone lover plays on
Where the little girl circles and the lone lover plays on

Walk the river
With moon and misery for company
I'll be on the other side
The other side, my honey
Your near murderous desire to fall in love
A fear for me it ain't written from above
Love's a gold dust, like sprinkling salt they say
Once it's been given, it can't be taken away
From the little girl that circles, as the lone lover plays on

From the little girl circles, as the lone lover plays on ...

119

The next Roman Britain

You never knew that the slavery of certainty would win
out
Till you had to crawl all down and out in dirty doubt
With the treachery of time you must now ride
To hammer out any remaining misplaced pride
Sharing confessional crumbs with the tramp by your side
While the decaying debris of youth breathes life into
your old age
His words still resounding "if in doubt follow the blonde,
she'll lead you to the next page
Where everything but concluding chapters have already
been written
For the ascension of a new king and the next Roman
Britain"

But who could substitute bountiful beauty for beauty all
abound?

The coast's collection of washed up artefacts are missing
having you around
And how can you trap a wingless bird that's never know
what it is to be free?
Will the serpent repent with a sip from the chalice you
have chosen for me?
Worried waves of plane fluid always rise to the top, so
sayeth the sage
His words still resound "if in doubt follow the blonde,
she'll lead you to the next page
Where everything but concluding chapters have already
been written
For the ascension of a new king and the next Roman
Britain"

© Ed Fram 2015

120

The poetic potion

I'll be addicted to his truth, wherever I'm taken by the poetic potion
To where red rivers have run dry and her tear could fill
an ocean
Where tongues are well-travelled, but only one language
is spoken
Where I see those left behind and how to death they've
awoken

I'll be covered in his truth, whenever I'm taken by the poetic potion
To when nihilism rules the sky and black is the only
emotion
When I feel your love as something that's now forever
broken
When you hand me dead flowers and an unused subway
token

Ah! To be at one with his truth, whoever is taken by the
poetic potion
For who can see what I've seen and not show devotion?
Who could defy a presence so fierce and yet soft-spoken?
Who would deny you the chance to have your heart un-
broken?

© Ed Fram 2015

121

The ragged road

Those most ancient of men
They had a point for each pyramid
Amid the wise you would hear again
"It won't take long for a smart man
To say something stupid!"
But you, fair to the end, to do as you did
Make for yourself no trouble round this bend
Keep on down the ragged road to the end
Then I'll know in you I have a friend

In you, I have a friend ...
Follow not the famous faces who scorch the land
Lending a hand but only for a while
Now upturned smiles for mile after mile
With interrogation masquerading as curiosity
With masks to hide their animosity
For no one likes a bad loser!
But as they turn away, we'll hear them say
"Some things remain nothing some of the time

But nothing stays nothing all of the time"
Then we'll know we're doing fine
Yes, we're doing just fine ...

See those most ancient of men
They had a point for each pyramid
Amid the wise you would hear again
"It won't take long for a smart man
To say something stupid!"
But you, fair to the end, to do as you did
Make for yourself no trouble round this bend
Keep on down the ragged road to the end
Then I'll know in you I have a friend
Yes, in you, I have a friend ...

122

The road to Singapore

They'll show you enough
to make you want them
Not so much that you won't
She told me death's like Rome
Every route leads you there
So come on over, call me home
Don't just stand and stare

'Tis the season to forget all reason
Brush the dust from baubles in your beard
Light up the tree, it's time to get weird
Look down to see faith don't come free
But for now keep singing, whoopie whoopie

Unapologetically accept the wisdom of the dwarfs
Stomping on snowflakes while above fires softly morph
Into the lord and the lady, oh so civilised!
But don't be fooled by their disguise
They're nostalgic for colourless hangings

Thinking they don't do it like they used to

Chocolates from Belgium
Jewels I never held 'em in much regard
(The stones are just too hard)
But give me red roses for my blue heart
I'll strike another pose and they'll call it art
Like scribbles on a community board
In praise of solitary pursuits
They'll take what you have stored
Leaving barefoot, after filling up their boots

Too young to die, too old for living
It must be lonely being so forgiving
Treasure's all around
But she searches for discarded dimes
From those early Roman times
His carriage is electric
His lady coughs coal
Return the pawn that you stole
Then lend me your eyes so I can see
How conspiracy lies beyond theory

Black is the colour I weep
Darkness where souls go to sleep
But as wet paint must soon run dry
The tide too will surely pass by
Like boats marooned in mud
Waiting to be rescued by the sea, their lifeblood
All around me that's what I see

But then again, it might just be me

Luck tried me on for size
She didn't like the fit
Like dignitaries from the four corners
Seen through the donkey's eyes
Just signatories hungry for honours
A masked ball for the wise
Bringing tales from tuppence
Now so disgraced
He ain't worth much more
Super-animals in his place

John took the Matthew across seas so far
We were so few, they as many as the stars
Men with nothing but a shadow's scent
To guide them on the road to Singapore
Won't you now return what I lent
What did you go and do that for?
Serving nudes improperly dressed
Who'll do anything you request
As long as you say please
But the sun will set as the seas will rise
Watch out that we ain't taken by surprise
For these days are surely numbered

They'll show you enough
to make you want them
Not so much that you won't
She told me death's like Rome

Every route leads you there
So come on over, call me home
Don't just stand and stare

123

The ruins of salvation

He walks around with time on his hands and memories
on his back
Fortune has favoured him, wherever he goes he carries it
in his sack
But he has no time for time wasters, unless they happen
to know
How to pass time more swiftly, when life's decidin' which
way to go ...

And though our eyes just met, between the twisted rainbow and the melting snow
I got this feeling that I should follow you, straight to the
main show
Where purple prisms collide with dreams of undying
death
Where everyone is shouting "tell us what else you got
left!"
Where I walk around with time on my hands and memories on my back

But fortune don't always favour the brave, it depends on
your line of attack ...

So lead me to the place where no man will cease to be
waiting
For the berry pickers and mermaid girls to quit their ges-
ticulating
At the cowboy and his seven white horses in a line so
proud
At the glamorous maiden and her silent stare she's wearing so loud
And speak to me softly of how you too once enjoyed the
same crowd
And how you now walk around with time on your hands
and memories on your back
Telling me how many storms a stone can weather, before
it begins to crack
But can fortune ever favour us, leaving the ruins of salvation on the other side of the track?

© Ed Fram 2015

124

The silent picture

You have no need for books, you read people instead
In this world all is fair but unequal,
you always said
Carrying on into a trap you've set yourself
Beyond where the priest's forgotten to cross himself
To you the face is known, the name is forgot
"One swing of the thurible, that's your lot!"
Taking with both hands
Saying "what else can one do?
I'm sent to recover lost lands
That could've belonged to you"

For he followed the ancient scripts, you beat him with
sticks
Yet no noise did he make, not a word passed his lips
The silent picture was the talk of the show
Yes, the silent picture was the talk of the show

They all love him now, but that's really no way to soften
the blow
You're holed in, so you'd better stop digging
Ring out the message in the homes of the unwilling
Adherents to a religion of little temptation
Where everything goes 'cept quiet contemplation
Now you're scouring scrawls from shelves dust-swept
Modern man is dead, Jesus wept
Modern man is dead, Jesus wept

He followed the ancient scripts, you beat him with sticks
Yet no noise did he make, not a word passed his lips
The silent picture was the talk of the show
Yes, the silent picture was the talk of the show

© Ed Fram 2015

125

The stillness of the night

If you're passing down that well-beaten path
Take this kiss over from me to hide my wrath
And pick up some flowers from near the craggy shore
Better than carryin' words like she ain't heard 'em before
And I'll be takin' my song on the road
The meaning's gone but the tongue ain't slowed
Yet there's no more searchin' for pleasure and applause
Even a ramblin' soul's sometimes got cause to pause
For what's missed in the stillness of the night
You ain't ever gettin' back to put right
No, you ain't ever gettin' it back to put right ...

It's too late when your name has been drawn
And the moon's been out long past the dawn
An unclaimed sign leavin' all to wonder who got there
first

The flag looks like it's yours, but the bearer is dying of
thirst
And the smuggler's bringing dahlias, thinking them her
favourite flowers
But she left with another a while ago, she got tired of
waitin' for hours
Yet what's missed in the stillness of the night
She ain't ever gettin' back to put right
No, she ain't ever gettin' it back to put right ...

Now the captain and his genius, he ain't really got much
to say
He stands between me and the sun, before headin' off on
his way
And just because she smiled back, it don't mean we're to-
gether, no
It depends on what's she's readin' and the kind of
weather, so
Catch the breeze while you can, no one can tell which
way she'll next go
When you finally get what you've been without, only
then will you know
That what's missed in the stillness of the night
Can't ever be gotten back to put right
No, it can't ever be gotten back to put right ...

© Ed Fram 2015

126

The way we used to be

Carry me long, carry me there
Carry me through from year to year
Carry me close, carry me brave
Carry me to where I'll be saved

How many stars must twinkle in your eyes
Till you will see the light?
How long must I wait for the sunrise
Now the night's out of sight?
How long must I look out the window
Before reaching for the door?
How many ways are there to show
I can't take being without you no more?

Take me to where you smiled for me
Take me to the way we used to be
Take me through the forgotten fields

Where death's a pain that no man feels

At a factory for their perceived perfection
With chimneys blasting ideas like confection
Everyone wants their tuppence counted, though the pot
can hold no more
There ain't nothing that can be done when they're
spilling out onto the floor
There you'll find me, trapped by a past I've never known
Thinking of nothing else but the time our house was a
home

Carry me long, carry me there
Carry me through from year to year
Carry me close, carry me brave
To where love is king and I'm its slave

Time called on the watch maker's apprentice
For how else could we end this?
But who knew they'd fly the big flag for a cause so small?
Those who'd walk away each time we call
Who'd carry on each time we fall
Who'd forget our name, like we didn't matter at all
No, not all jokes are meant to be funny
And sometimes sorrow's as sweet as honey

So I'll take you to where you smiled for me
I'll take you to the way we used to be
I'll take you through the forgotten fields
I'll take you to where numbed hearts feel

© Ed Fram 2016

Think nothing of it

Throw your robes to the floor, think nothing of it
Change to a creature born in the mind of Ovid
You who are so used to wondering naked in exile
Hands filled with a poem and an error to reconcile
To answer the critics from a time that has yet come
To guard governor's secrets and all you're running from

The showman and his jealous wife, carrying a symphony
of sneezes
He takes no pleasure from life, she just does as she pleases
The tracks and carriages are all lined up, you're tuned in
to an unmanned frequency
Hand over your ticket to the devil you know, we're all
just seeking some consistency
Running for a train that's going the wrong way outta
here
But any way away from you is never wrong, ain't it clear?

Throw your robes to the floor, think nothing of it

Change to a creature born in the mind of Ovid
Your unashamed touch so faint and fair is designed to
bruise and to blush
You're hiding all the cards underneath your chair, but I'm
declaring a royal flush
Wrap your tongue 'round words you don't know the
meaning of, but think nothing of it
Listen to me whispering them back to you, for I will always love you too, my beloved ...

© Ed Fram 2015

128

Tinged in blue

To live free in the past, you must let go of what's gone
You must also know that when something ain't off, it's
on
The ghosts are glowing so garish, they'll be visited upon
you too
Let the reluctant speaker say his piece, he's at the recep-
tion waiting for you
Your smile to him looks real enough, though it's still
tinged in blue ...

The cutlery will clatter, the odd couple continue to chat-
ter
They'll solve the riotous riddle and nothing else will mat-
ter
But around the table, where the circling birds once flew
The professor and his arguments are now in full view
Your mind to him looks real enough, though it's still
tinged in blue ...

No I have no proof, it's just sometimes I get this sense
That to be let in, you must use thirteen in a sentence
It'll be fine as long as you know what it's in reference to
You don't have to see eye to eye, but you must share the
same world view
Your voice to her sounds soft enough, though it's still
tinged in blue ...

It's all around to those in the know, it's what the rest seek
out the most
Those with little to send and receive are guarding the
telegraph post
For the collage of the curator is rated up to and including
the debut
And with each step she takes away, her presence gets
nearer for you
Your heart to her feels real enough, though it's still
tinged in blue ...

© Ed Fram 2015

129

To see that you sleep well

By the frozen lake, 'neath the sky's crystal chill
Our hearts were warmed by eternal embers
For just a moment the wind stood still
And we walked carefree, like we'd have endless Decem-
bers
Suffering feeds the soul, you always say
But I know I'll be at the table some day
To write away your precious pain, till the ink runs dry!
And I'll sing you this lonely lullaby, till the angels cry!
To see that you sleep well, my love
To see that you sleep well ...

Their baskets you filled with plenty from the fruit tree
farm
The belly aches, though your lips never touched nothin'
but trouble

Your arms were strong but your hands never knew to
harm
Silver-linings scraped with each pull of the rake, cloud
castles turned to rubble
Suffering feeds the soul, you always say
But I know I'll be at the table some day
To write away your precious pain, till the ink runs dry!
And I'll sing you this lonely lullaby, till the angels cry!
To see that you sleep well, my love
To see that you sleep well ...

The belt was bended my way, to be beaten and forever
banished
And to turn your labouring hand to loving him instead
Your beauty stays within and the bruises long ago did
vanish
Though my tongue is tortured still by all the words we
left unsaid
Suffering feeds the soul, you always say
But I know I'll be at the table some day
To write away your precious pain, till the ink runs dry!
And I'll sing you this lonely lullaby, till the angels cry!
To see that you sleep well, my love
To see that you sleep well ...

We'd still be travellin' on the sails of that spinning mill
The trees snapped like matchsticks by a hungry hurricane
overfed
In that place, where the wind had once stood still
On this day, you walked in white and the rivers ran red

Suffering feeds the soul, you always say
But I know I'll be at the table some day
To write away your precious pain, till the ink runs dry!
And I'll sing you this lonely lullaby, till the angels cry!
To see that you sleep well, my love
To see that you sleep well ...

© Ed Fram 2015

130

To where happiness is easy

My words to you, they're forever lost
I'm sure I wrote them all down
Still I ain't counting the cost
Like the reluctant king, pleased to be without a crown
For there ain't no use for pen and pad
When thinking of the one I love most
Whether I be happy or sad
You light up the bleakest night coast
And in the light of what we know
Shines forth the darkness of what we don't
So let's meet at that ancient place, let's put on that show
We'll travel to the opposite house, where others won't
To where happiness is easy
To where happiness is easy

Away from the viper rooms, where they speak of dens of
distrust

They grew up disgracefully, yet confidently claim to be
upper crust
While outside the blue swans glide on fear and what's
near instead
As the intelligentsia browse books on how to appear
well-read
Some hate what life has done to them
Others hate what they have done with life
But we'll travel to the opposite house, where others
won't
To where happiness is easy
To where happiness is easy

© Ed Fram 2015

131

Too lonely a silence

He didn't know it
But I could tell he was a poet
You just had to look at his fingertips
Pristine wisps of vapour at the lips
Each time he spoke
This ain't no ordinary bloke

But it was too lonely a silence
For any one man to bear
The sound of the street dance
Gone as it came, into thin air

That's when she came to me
Like a vision from above
If I didn't know any better
I'd have called it love

She's a slave to all she's mastered
A master by slaving away

On a Minnesota farm, last I heard
Working double for half pay

And what of me, you ask politely
When are you coming back?
I'll follow the poet, he's always right on track
Before the storm blows out
Once I figure how to be without
Something approaching happiness

© Ed Fram 2017

132

Two and a half steps

I'm still wearing the scars
But I've forgotten how to feel
You got them big fancy cars
The judge will hear your appeal

The fervent and the gentile
They all like your style
They'd like to write like you do
I'm hoping you'll inspire me too

The bridge might still be standing
I crossed it blind to where I'd be landing
But I'll wear my boots into the ground
Before handing over another pound

I'm two and a half steps in
Your deeds scattered upon the seas
All the seats are taken
But can you meet my needs?

Van Gogh, he lent me his ear
I taught him how to walk through walls
The boundless books are here
The pre-Raphaelite relics are in the hall

The over-privileged tramp
He's chewing on your smokes
His mail don't need a stamp
We all laugh at his jokes

A lifetime seeking order
In ephemeral works
Meet me at the border
While the judge just smirks

© Ed Fram 2017

133

Unsold and sold

Her touch is untested, the record's still playin' broken
The window to the street and its seasons was left open
In here, it's emptied of spoiled smoke and heady hopin'
"Don't turn to me with feelings so true, I'm heartless, do
you not recall?"
Though fates may be twisted and turned on a look, to be
in it for the long haul
But who can satisfy the arrogance that comes from age-
ing just right?
Who will be there but the darkness to bid you farewell
and goodnight?

Your story front and back runs to two hundred and
twenty-two
Never was more written about so little and so few
We just met, but I'm mentioned in there along with the
raven too
And with his pages, the shaman fans the flames in the
forests of Sherwood

He steals his verses from the rich and poor, he gets his
matches from Robin Hood
But who can satisfy the arrogance that comes from age-
ing just right?
Who will be there but the darkness to bid him farewell
and goodnight?

Now it's endlessly just one, there's no use for this counting calendar
Not even for the sun, for all's washed clear in leaves of
lavender
And there's nothing new for saving, even less that might
be old
Just liquid gold ripples running through the streets unpa-
trolled
And a sign 'neath your boarded window reading "Unsold
and sold"
But who can satisfy the arrogance that comes from age-
ing just right?
Who will be there but the darkness to bid you farewell
and goodnight?

© Ed Fram 2015

134

Uprise

Uprise fair sun, uprise to behold the daylight rose!
Shine hereon the dewdrop, shine o my morning jewel!
And curse the night that ordains her light to a close
Foreshadowing evening tears, so cavernous and so cruel.
A heart stopped unforgivingly
The flower plucked before the bloom.
Ashes scattered so lovingly
Before the crow has time to croon ...

Come forth blackened angel of doom!
Speak for the tongueless, tormentors of mendacious minds!
Come forth to relieve us of our gloom!
Devour the devoid of form and those of an unworldly kind!
For the light in you has been snuffed out at the close of the
longest day
The wicked wick of a candlestick, shan't be revived no mat-
ter how long you now may pray ...

Uprise fair sun, uprise to behold the daylight rose!
Shine hereon the dewdrop, shine o my morning jewel!
And curse the night that ordains her light to a close
Foreshadowing evening tears, so cavernous and so cruel.
A heart stopped unforgivingly
The flower plucked before the bloom.
Ashes scattered so lovingly
Before the crow has time to croon …

© Ed Fram 2019

135

When freedom comes

Brush off the dawn dust
Say adieu to the dew
It ain't love it ain't lust
Just your arms overdue
the burden of caring

Everyone relies on someone
At least some of the time
Just make sure you ain't leaning on me
When you think I'm doing just fine

So quit horsing around
in crooked stables
Singing songs ain't sound
With food to decorate tables
untouched by the starving

I better be quick
See 'em before they go

I better be quick
See 'em before I'm laid low

Now why you actin' all mysterious?
I can't figure it out
Why you lookin' so serious?
Seriously making me doubt

Go home, go on home my honey
Go find a place to belong
I dunno if it's sad or funny
That I ain't right and you ain't wrong

And I'll see you by the gate
Pail of milk by the quarter
It ain't choice, it ain't fate
Charity, I never bought her
A free-for-all
(Till all are free)

© Ed Fram 2016

136

Where shall we go? (Ballad of the bells)

The bells have sounded their all, I'm told
And the last of sheep have broken from the fold
The church tower a broken timepiece
memories from a time now gone
All that remains from that time when only the truth
shone
And where shall we go, now that the bells' pealing's
ceased?

The bells that signalled the end of war
Carrying back those you adore
The bells that sung of harvest feast
Telling of fields with more than empty straw to release
The bells that cried for the lover's death
Now must sound for themselves, bereft
The bells that once sealed our love
Now only heard by those above

The bells that played sweet Christmastide chime
Now silenced by man's heathen rhymes

Ah the bells have sounded their all, I'm told
And the last of sheep have broken from the fold
The church tower a broken timepiece, memories from a
time now gone
All that remains from that time when only the truth
shone
And where shall we go, now that the bells' pealing's
ceased?
Where shall we go, when all around lies desolate, de-
ceased?

© Ed Fram 2015

137

Young yearners

Hoofbeats pounding round your door
Fallen branches are trees unto themselves
The young yearners are tangled on the floor
As Shakespeare's sonnets gather dust on the shelves ...

But you forget to remember
How I remember to forget
You can't stand how I defend her
Avoiding all the traps you set

Me with my mandolin by my side
Your words like water, how they flow
We're speaking in tongues that collide
Leaving me with no other place to go

You better make art to live with eternally
For the famous unbelonger I have not yet seen
He's down where the souls lie lifelessly
I've spoken to one who's been

Hoofbeats pounding round your door
Fallen branches are trees unto themselves
The young yearners are tangled on the floor
As Shakespeare's sonnets gather dust on the shelves ...

© Ed Fram 2020

www.ingramcontent.com/pod-product-compliance
Lightning Source LLC
Chambersburg PA
CBHW070726030726
47601CB00007B/273/J